Praise for *Against the Storm*

"Finally, a leadership book that treats reality, context and psychology as the core ingredients of leading well in uncertain times."

—Alex Lazarus
Business Psychologist;
Founder & CEO, Lazarus & Maverick

"Against the Storm *is an essential and practical guide for leading when the ground keeps shifting."*

—Sanyin Siang
CEO Advisor and Duke University Professor

"This book takes us on a journey of transformation of leadership to what is needed and necessary for the modern world."

—Dr. Diane Ryan
CEO, International Coaching Federation

"*In* Against the Storm, *Tom Kolditz and Mariana Khomitska translate decades of experience in high-stakes uncertainty into clear, practical guidance for leading when the path forward is unclear."*

—Dr. Diane Ryan
Lecturer,
the Fletcher School, Tufts University

"Tom Kolditz and Mariana Khomitska have written the leadership book our moment demands."

—Scott Osman
CEO, 100 Coaches Agency

"Against the Storm *equips you to lead when knowledge is partial, time is short, and lives could be lost.*"

—Bill Sherman
Author of *The Thought Leadership Handbook* and
COO Thought Leadership Leverage

"Against the Storm *is one of those books that has come along at the right time with the right message for leaders today.*"

—Sarah McArthur
Editor in Chief,
Leader to Leader Journal

"*In* Against the Storm, *Tom Kolditz and Mariana Khomistka give leaders concrete tools to navigate rapid change and to foster adaptability, initiative, and resilience under pressure. An indispensable resource for leaders at every level.*"

—Alison Levine
American mountaineer, motivational speaker,
leadership consultant, author of *On the Edge: Leadership Lessons from Mount Everest and Other Extreme Environments*

"*Kolditz and Khomitska write an exceptionally practical leadership book filled with useful techniques for leaders to build resilience and adaptability in times of crisis and uncertainty.*"

—Cynthia Cherrey
President and CEO International Leadership Association

AGAINST THE STORM

AGAINST THE STORM

How True Leaders Prevail When the World Shakes

TOM KOLDITZ &
MARIANA KHOMITSKA

WILEY

Published by John Wiley & Sons, Inc., Hoboken, New Jersey.

For general information on our other products and services or for technical support, please contact our Customer Care Department within the United States at (800) 762-2974, outside the United States at (317) 572-3993 or fax (317) 572-4002.

Wiley also publishes its books in a variety of electronic formats. Some content that appears in print may not be available in electronic formats. For more information about Wiley products, visit our web site at www.wiley.com.

Library of Congress Cataloging-in-Publication Data has been applied for:

ISBN: 9781394387793 (cloth)
ISBN: 9781394387809 (ePub)
ISBN: 9781394387816 (ePDF)

Cover Design: Wiley
Cover Images: iconiyo/stock.adobe.com, MiaStendal/stock.adobe.com
SKY10163235_072226

Portions of this text were drafted with assistance of Gemini by Google. The AI tool helped organize our ideas, suggest alternative phrasing for complex concepts, and improve clarity and conciseness throughout the writing process. All AI-generated content was carefully reviewed, edited, and approved. The final analysis, conclusions, and interpretations represent our own views and expertise. We take full responsibility for the content and accuracy of this work.

Contents

Foreword

These days if you think you know what's going on and what's going to happen, it's quite possible you haven't understood the situation.

What work is, what employment is, what relationships are, what politics is, what technology is, what the environment is, what power is, what the world order is … it's all up for grabs in a way that no one's ever seen before. Each of those different spheres may or may not be in a moment of crisis at any one time. But all of them, singularly and combined, are in a perpetual state of uncertainty. The good news is that you have a deeply biological way of responding during uncertain times. The bad news is that your brain-wired preference for fight, flight, freeze, or fawn isn't going to work as a sustainable leadership response.

When I've found myself in times of uncertainty, moments that certainly do not have the complexity or gravity that the authors Tom Kolditz and Mariana Khomitska have experienced, I've found myself seeking to hold the paradox of staying grounded and also staying light. Being grounded means having your feet in the mud of reality. What's the data that I have? What signal can I discern amongst the noise? What do I know to be true … about the context, the challenge at hand, the other people involved, and my own strengths and weaknesses? When things are uncertain, we're flooded by emotions and opinions, feelings and judgments. When we're overwhelmed by what's incoming, returning to the moment and discerning what's true is staying grounded. At the same time, you're seeking lightness. That often means the capacity to generate new possibilities and options.

It's all too common to come up with a single solution that quickly hardens into the only solution. Once you've got a good grip on that solution, it's hard to put it down, let alone pick another and weigh it up. When the situation feels urgent and serious, staying quicksilver enough to explore new ways of responding is staying light. Both being grounded and staying light requires curiosity. What do I know to be true? What's possible from here? And what else? Curiosity is a meta leadership skill, one that unlocks other leadership attributes.

Tom and Marina have written a book that's deeply grounded in the reality of leading in a time of uncertainty. Tom served as a brigadier general for the US military and taught at West Point. Mariana has been an active, professional leader developer in Ukraine. In addition to their own hard-won wisdom, they've woven insights from interviews with business, government, and military experts throughout.

The chapter about creating agency was the one that rang loudest for me. Yes, of course, you build your own capacity to be in the midst of uncertainty and crisis and respond as a leader. You also must build capacity and courage in others. At the best of times walking a line that's not micromanaging on one hand nor free-range "find your vibe" on the other is difficult. During times of stress, it's even harder. But it's an utter waste of time to build capacity for working through uncertainty in yourself, if no one around had the same opportunity to do similar work.

You might know the term "antifragile," made popular in Nassim Nicholas Taleb's book of the same name. His argument is that it's not enough for systems to be robust or resilient.

That's somehow a passive response to the situation. "Antifragile" declares you need to build something that can actively meet the moment. For you and the people you lead and influence, this book gives you practical ways to meet this uncertain moment and do some good.

—By Michael Bungay Stanier

Introduction

The world we now face is full of uncertainty.

This book is oriented on both crisis and uncertainty, so it makes sense to discuss their relationship to each other. Uncertainty and crisis overlap considerably. The relationship between crisis and uncertainty is interdependent and cyclical, with a crisis acting as a powerful force that significantly amplifies existing uncertainty. Either can come first.

A crisis, by its very nature as an unexpected, nonroutine, and threatening event, immediately erodes predictability and control. Crises are often so new, complex, and rapidly unfolding that accurate, complete information is scarce or conflicting. This creates a severe lack of knowledge (epistemological uncertainty) about what is happening, who is responsible, and the extent of the damage. Crises often defy established routines and processes, meaning that past experience is a poor guide for the future. This creates uncertainty about how to respond and what the ultimate impact will be. The core of a crisis is a perceived or actual threat to an organization's, community's, or individual's ultimate goals (e.g., survival, stability). The doubt about whether these goals will be met is itself a source of profound uncertainty.

In essence, a crisis is defined by a spike in uncertainty. High uncertainty feeds back into the crisis, making it more difficult to manage and potentially worsening its impact. When information is incomplete and the outcomes are unpredictable, leaders and individuals can face analysis paralysis, where they delay decisions, or alternatively make reactive, ill-informed decisions. Uncertainty triggers fear and anxiety in people, leading to stress, emotional exhaustion, and a breakdown in morale. This can hinder a coordinated, effective response. In uncertain times, stakeholders (employees, customers, the public) look to leaders for clear direction and reassurance. A perceived failure to provide this certainty erodes trust, which is critical for compliance and support during the crisis.

One of the primary purposes of this book is to pass along leadership tools for crisis management. Effective crisis management is fundamentally about reducing uncertainty to restore a sense of control and stability. Key strategies focus on minimizing the effects of uncertainty:

- **Transparency and Communication:** Providing clear, consistent, and honest communication is the primary tool for reducing uncertainty. Leaders must acknowledge the ambiguity while sharing what is known and what steps are being taken. In later chapters, we discuss key communications techniques in meetings and other forms of interaction.
- **Decisive Action:** Making rapid, well-informed decisions—even on incomplete information—demonstrates control and can prevent the crisis from escalating, thereby reducing future uncertainty. We discuss how to engage and involve others in the key decisions that leaders must make with minimal knowledge and information. Empowerment is often a critical element of leadership in uncertainty and crisis, and this book shows how to initiate and support such empowerment.

- **Scenario Planning:** Proactively identifying potential risks and developing contingency plans provides a structured framework for unexpected events, limiting the shock and uncertainty when a crisis hits. We discuss key tools for controlling the quality and accuracy of scenario planning and execution, to include red teaming to identify problems, and the rehearsal of future scenario executions.
- **Adaptive Learning:** Crises force organizations to continuously learn and adjust their approach as new information emerges, creating new, more resilient operational models that are better equipped to handle future unpredictable events. This book reveals ways to establish and maintain a learning organization.

Leadership in uncertainty requires specific techniques. The purpose of this book is to describe those techniques sufficiently so that they can be immediately applied in both business and personal lives.

As authors, we both have considerable experience at training leaders who must work in chaos, crisis, and uncertainty. Thomas Kolditz wrote a book that details what we can all learn from people who lead in dangerous contexts, *In Extremis Leadership*. One of the primary purposes of that work was to teach others how to lead in uncertainty, uncertainty being a primary quality of all dangerous contexts. Mariana Khomitska has been an active, professional leader developer in Ukraine, where there is maximum uncertainty about not only the future of business, but of the existence of the country itself. Her employment with DTEK, Ukraine's largest employer, and with Ni-X, a global technology firm, has placed her in charge of showing leaders how to move forward into an unstable, uncertain, dangerous future.

The Unprecedented Need for a Guidebook to Leadership in an Age of Uncertainty

In an era defined by rapid-fire technological disruption, fractured geopolitical landscapes, and persistent economic volatility, the publication of a book on leading in uncertain times has become more than just timely—it is an essential resource for navigating the complexities of the modern world. The very nature of leadership is being redefined as traditional; hierarchical models prove inadequate for the challenges of today and the unforeseen trials of tomorrow.

The current global climate, marked by a confluence of destabilizing forces, underscores the urgent need for a new leadership paradigm. We are contending with the pervasive integration of AI, which is reshaping industries and job markets at an astonishing pace. Simultaneously, geopolitical tensions and trade disputes create a volatile and unpredictable environment for international business. Add to this the lingering economic anxieties stemming from inflation and supply chain vulnerabilities, and the result is a landscape where certainty is a scarce commodity.

This book, dedicated to leading through such turbulence, will serve as a critical guide for leaders and decision-makers at all levels. It would offer frameworks and strategies for not only surviving but thriving amid ambiguity. One of the primary benefits of such a work would be its focus on **resilience and adaptability**. Leaders are no longer expected to have all the answers; instead, their value lies in their ability to foster a culture of learning, experimentation, and quick adaptation. This book will provide actionable advice on how to build resilient teams that can weather shocks and pivot effectively in the face of unexpected change.

Yet the contributions of the book go far beyond us, the two authors. In addition to the more than 60 years of leadership experience we have, we have added the perspective of many leadership experts. We interviewed them and asked questions that related to the conditions of, and the execution of, our leadership techniques. These experts include the following:

- Alan Murray, formerly CEO of Fortune Media, current leader of the Wall Street Journal Leadership Institute.
- Lina Hidalgo, twice elected judge (top executive) of Harris County (Houston Texas), a county so sizable that its GDP exceeds that of New Zealand. Lina leads more than 4.85 million people, with a $2.6 billion dollar budget, and responsibility for all crisis events including hurricanes, chemical spills, major fires, and other disasters.
- Dr. Mark Hertling, a retired three-star general, formerly a military analyst for CNN, leadership expert, and former senior vice president at Florida Hospital. He served in the US Army for nearly 40 years, commanding at every level from tank platoon to Field Army. His career included leading the 1st Armored Division during the Iraq surge and commanding US Army Europe, where he oversaw more than 60,000 soldiers.
- Dr. Bernard "Bernie" Banks, retired one-star general, former head of the Department of Behavioral Sciences and Leadership at West Point and former head of leadership at the Kellogg School of Business at Northwestern University, currently the director of the Ann & John Doerr Institute for New Leaders at Rice University.
- Mark S. Thompson, chairman of the Chief Executive Alliance, LLC, and ranked as the *World's #1 CEO Coach* and Coaching Legends Hall of Fame by the Thinkers50. In collaboration with his coauthor, Byron Loflin, Nasdaq Head of Board Excellence, Mark leads High Performance C-Team

Readiness programs based on their Harvard Business Review book, *CEO Readiness: Success Strategies for Succession in the C-Suite*.

As an example, consider how Alan Murray characterizes how uncertainty changes leadership:

> I believe uncertainty changes the fundamental model of leadership ... to the twentieth century model where the leader gives orders and by follows, you have to Power the people on the front line to react circumstances, when circumstance change and so inevitably, the leader has be much more about inspiration, about guarding, about providing the North Star, and much more willing to empower the team to end the right solution.

Furthermore, in times of uncertainty, **clear and transparent communication** becomes paramount. A book on this subject would almost certainly emphasize the importance of honest and frequent dialogue to manage anxiety, build trust, and maintain morale. When the future is unclear, employees look to their leaders for a sense of stability and purpose. This type of book can equip leaders with the communication tools necessary to provide that grounding, even when they don't have all the information.

Another critical theme such a book would likely explore is the **psychology of leadership in high-stakes environments**. Uncertainty can breed fear and paralysis. A well-researched book would delve into the cognitive biases that can cloud judgment in times of crisis and offer strategies for maintaining a clear and rational perspective. It could provide insights into fostering psychological safety, empowering teams to take calculated risks, and leading with empathy and compassion—qualities that are often the first casualties of a crisis-driven mindset. The impact of uncertainty on stress in both leaders and followers is characterized well by Lina Hidalgo, whose unique role places her on top of every significant crisis in and outside the city of Houston, Texas:

> And if just the fact of uncertainty is causing you stress, you know that's just an additional thing to have to think about. I think now what I've learned is to just accept uncertainty as you know, part of the cost of doing business in terms of, you know, you just and really trying to imbue that in my team. Oftentimes, you know, they'll be, they'll be really, really hopeful about an outcome. And it's like, okay, we can, we can hope for something, but let's be realistic about the possibility that that outcome pans out and then, you know, if it doesn't, we say thank you and move on and on to the next thing. Another way that it affects my work is, obviously there are no clear answers for a lot of what we do, there's externalities that you can never think of, just in, I think in all fields, but certainly in government, and so just being able to have folks on the team and to feel comfortable myself with making decisions with information that you know it's never going to be anywhere near perfect.

Ultimately, a book on leading in uncertain times is not just a manual for crisis management; it is a roadmap for fostering **innovation and opportunity**. Periods of great disruption are also periods of great change, offering a fertile ground for new ideas and new ways of operating. By providing leaders with the tools to navigate the challenges, such a book also empowers them to seize the opportunities that uncertainty inevitably creates. It is an investment in a future where leaders are not just reactors to a volatile world, but proactive shapers of a more resilient and prosperous tomorrow. Much of the purpose of business schools is to create such a future orientation. Lieutenant General Mark Hertling is clear about the importance of leaders understanding both the challenges and the opportunities of uncertainty and crisis, and especially the need for preparation in front of possible outcomes:

> Well, … I'll share with you what I talk about in our MBA program, because I teach a segment like you do on crisis leadership … I learned a whole lot about the deliberate planning process and what was in the military's what people call the war plans, but what we call contingency plans, and doing the review of the contingencies plans with all of the combatant commanders and [Secretary of Defense Donald] Rumsfeld was an experience, quite frankly, he spent, he would have the four stars come in, lay out their plans and then talk about them. And he literally spent an hour or so, or sometimes more, questioning their assumptions to their plans, which is the first thing in a contingency plan. So, you know, it's the start of a cycle of making assumptions about what might happen in the future that would turn into a crisis, or something we would be unprepared for. So it's a starting point to make sure you are prepared for what might slap you in the face. In combat, I always had a sign above the map board in my [Tactical Operations Center] that said, "What are they doing that we don't know about? What haven't we prepared for?"

Similarly, the famous CEO coach Mark C. Thompson reveals the need for leaders in uncertainty to make decisions regardless:

> And under circumstances where there is never adequate data, and you can pretend there is, and you know, you and I go into very high quality, very rigorous academic institutions. And then, having been with the rigor of highly competitive … corporate environments not having enough data and not having always the evidence to make those choices is kind of the most dangerous and the most rewarding crucible of every leader at the top of the house ….

Crisis is very common, not a one-off occurrence but a constant challenge in our lives. We have spoken on this topic hundreds of times. In most cases, the presentation began by asking the audience to raise their hands to the following experiences:

- Have you ever been physically attacked or shot at before?
- Have you ever participated in an extreme sport, like skydiving, helicopter skiing, half piping, or scuba diving?
- Do you have military, police, or firefighting experience?
- Have you experienced a crisis where your life was threatened?
- Have you experienced a death in your organization?
- Have you ever been part of a government or organization in crisis?
- Have you ever been responsible or accountable for the death of another person?

In every case, someone raised their hand at one or more of these crises, with the exception of being responsible or accountable for the death of another person. That particular question was sometimes not a part of the audience's experience. In other instances, such as speaking to physicians, hospitals, fire fighters, police, military, veterans, EMTs, and a host of other critical occupations, it was so common as to be held by the majority of the attendees. The point made: crises are not a rarity. They are a routine part of our lives. Another example of this came from a presentation to 150 executives from a well-known, highly successful pharmaceutical company. Tom polled them and asked, "Are you, at this time, experiencing a professional crisis, a personal crisis, or both." Precisely 50% reported living in some form, or multiple forms, of crisis at that time.

Uncertainty is even more common than crisis. Crisis assumes a credible threat. Uncertainty assumes a lack of information, with anything from disaster to success rolling toward the outcome. Uncertainty is dealing with unknowns, jumped on here by the director of the Ann & John Doerr Institute for New Leaders at Rice University:

> I believe (uncertainty is) being cognizant of what's transpiring in three buckets, known knowns, known unknowns and the unknown unknowns for the known knowns. How do you act on that? For the known unknowns? How do you seek to turn those into known knowns? So we know that there's information we need to get access to right now. We don't have it. What's the best way of getting access to that information so we can leverage it, and then you've got the unknown unknowns. So how do you keep doing an environmental scan to say is anything popping up that we haven't accounted for, and once it does come on our radar, how do we then start to put it into one of those other buckets of known, unknown or known known, but having good environmental scans so that you can start moving stuff down that pipeline from unknown unknowns to unknown knowns to known knowns, which is where we act, had the greatest fidelity that allows you to start navigating those things in a more informed manner and in a systemic manner.

Leadership that is effective in uncertain times is equally effective in times of relative stability. As you read through the chapters, you'll become aware of the connections between uncertainty and the leadership techniques described. You'll recognize how they build trust and how they manage the anxiety and fear caused by uncertainty. You'll find that they are ways to better organizations without resolving uncertainty or eliminating crisis. They give you, as the leader, better control as needed in response to the pressures of uncertainty, the confusion of chaos, and the threats of crises. But, importantly, all the characteristics of the chapters are also equally effective when uncertainty and crisis are not apparent. Each of the leadership techniques is useful across an array of circumstances, challenging or not. As one might suspect, a significant part of leading in conditions of uncertainty is to reduce or eliminate it.

The opposite, however, is not true. There are many actions taken by leaders in routine circumstances that give the leader power, control, and influence *then*. It is not the case, however, that such behaviors will work well when the heat is on. Why is that? The answer is simple. When things are going well, and not stirred by uncertainty or crisis, people are willing to put up with all sorts of poor leadership. In straightforward circumstances, people often obey leaders whether they trust them or not. Yet in uncertainty and crisis, trust becomes the coin of the realm, and its importance places a demand on leaders. In routine circumstances, people follow the guidance of leaders and assume that proper outcomes will follow. But uncertainty and the pressures in crisis take away the ease of assumption. That's when confidence in the leader must be earned rather than assumed.

How This Book Is Structured

> Ideas are easy, execution is everything, and it takes a team to win.
>
> —John Doerr

Our book provides an understanding of how uncertainty and crisis impact our lives. It is not, however, a philosophical "idea" book—instead, it provides a host of useful and specific leadership techniques that you will be able to use immediately to improve the quality of your leadership—execution is everything.

Here is how the book is structured. Part I explores the crucible of crisis, showing how external disruption tests leaders, reveals organizational weaknesses, and sets the stage for transformation. It contains the following:

- **Chapter 1:** The first chapter lays out details of the nature of uncertainty and crisis. It describes the key elements of a volatile world—political, economic, health-related, societal shifts, predictable versus unpredictable uncertainties—taking the reader into the reality of the world in which we live.
- **Chapter 2:** This chapter is a description of how crisis and uncertainty affect the people experiencing them. Sustainability, resilience, and adaptability in the face of crisis and uncertainty impact all elements of our personal and professional lives. It is informed by business experiences in Ukraine at the start of the Russian invasion. Such conditions affect companies, nonprofits, teams, and families. Uncertainty and crisis are common conditions, given economic uncertainties, unanticipated occurrences, changes (positive and negative) to relationships, medical diagnoses, and many other turn of events. It sets the stage not only for discussions involving work, but personal challenges as well—everything in the book can be applied in both the professional and personal lives of leaders. Every part of a leader's life is influenced by uncertainty and crisis, and this chapter forwards the use of specific techniques to help manage that.
- **Chapter 3:** Chapter 3 delves into the psychology of crisis leadership, of leading in extraordinary levels of uncertainty. It depicts the emotional resilience of both leaders and followers in wartime Ukraine, offering readers a unique view of how emotions influence life and work. It is important that leaders understand how emotions and emotional intelligence affect their influence when people are afraid.

Part II focuses on the internal shift in mindset and human-centered leadership behaviors that enable leaders to adapt, guide, and sustain teams effectively in uncertainty:

- **Chapter 4:** This chapter explores the internal shift leaders must make to be effective in volatile environments. It is a treatise on how leaders must adapt to levels of uncertainty and crisis that flood their lives. Mini cases from both Ukraine and all of our experiences with the COVID-19 pandemic carry leaders forward with their understanding of how to change—and in some ways, how to stay consistent in their influence.
- **Chapter 5:** This chapter addresses the human side of leadership in uncertain contexts. It reveals how leaders best communicate, make decisions with minimal information, and how the best leaders balance human needs with business imperatives. These points are detailed through vivid real-world examples, including wartime Ukraine and the challenges to supply chain management after the COVID-19 crisis.

Part III provides practical, immediately applicable leadership tools and techniques that readers can use individually to strengthen their effectiveness in real-world situations:

- **Chapter 6:** This chapter explains how to handle meetings in times of uncertainty and crisis. More than half of the people in an organization feel that the best way to gather information is through meetings. For that reason, uncertainty or crisis has a significant impact on meetings. This chapter will enhance a leader's ability to manage meetings during uncertainty, maximize communication and collective understanding, control disruptive antagonists, and continue to build optimism, confidence, and trust. The application of what is taught in this chapter can be immediate.

- **Chapter 7:** This chapter describes how to take steps to recognize the approach of catastrophic events, and to eliminate or minimize their impact. Uncertainty, chaos, and crisis all represent limits on information and therefore make it more likely that a catastrophic event will occur with little or no warning. While such an occurrence cannot be completely eliminated, it can often be uncovered and controlled with a minimal amount of work. We take the readers through how to create and interpret a technique called a pre-mortem. The pre-mortem technique is useful for intercepting major problems not normally identified by the organization. It is also a confirmed process for developing intuition in rising leaders. In our experience, the higher you go in leadership roles, the more decisions must be made through the application of intuitive judgment. Given that, it is important that there are ways to exercise and improve intuitive judgment. Chapter 7 does just that.
- **Chapter 8:** This chapter teaches how to delegate and empower people in conditions of uncertainty and crisis. Often when many leaders recognize the informational limitations of uncertainty, they tend to slow down, close doors, and limit the independence of the people who work for them. That is almost always a mistake. When asked about actions in uncertainty and crisis, leadership experts recommend more delegation and empowerment of employees, rather than holding back. Chapter 8 teaches how to expand delegation in such a way as to encourage empowerment, eliminate micromanagement, but establish reasonable control and give guidance to those who are accomplishing operations. Learning to describe one's intent as a leader stands as the best way to encourage improvisation and initiative without giving up the control essential to keeping the focus

on the leader's agenda, not giving up control. Intent statements are often composed as part of a plan, so that when the plan becomes ineffective or unworkable, clear intent allows people to continue to operate, rather than waiting for a revised plan. Intent statements are not merely a way to empower others. Their formulation is also a way to confirm the guidance you receive from your boss, an excellent form of "read back" that not only validates the intent of the person one is working for, but gives the opportunity for leaders to share intent for immediate execution. Chapter 8 creates the conditions for superb delegation, careful clarification, and empowered action—all excellent features of great leadership.

- **Chapter 9:** This chapter teaches leaders how to prevent a flawed plan, in conditions of uncertainty, from being mistakenly adopted. Planning staff work hard to not only formulate a good plan, but to sell it to the leaders who wanted the plan built. They are highly committed to their work, which sets the conditions for problems to be overlooked or even passed over. Chapter 9 describes how to use red teams, which are small leader-appointed groups, independent of the planning staff, and whose only job is to find fault with the plan. Leaders who use red teams are far more likely to discover problems in a plan *before* it is adopted, either fixing or eliminating those problems.
- **Chapter 10:** This chapter teaches a leader how to best ensure the successful execution of a plan once it is adopted. There is much that a leader can do to assist in the execution of a plan, and conversely, there is much a leader can do to get in the way. Chapter 10 lays out ways for leaders to contribute to execution by creating operational rehearsals. Such rehearsals allow for the testing of most—and sometimes

all—of the features of a plan, in real time. It also shows how leaders sometimes give the operators too little time for their planning and the rehearsals. Leaders who apply the lessons in Chapter 10 are likely to have the smooth execution of plans, products, and projects.

- **Chapter 11:** This chapter reveals how a leader can create or maintain a learning organization that improves over time in uncertainty and crisis. Too often, leaders react to uncertainty or crisis by holding back on organizational development by focusing on only the present, rather than the future, of the organization. Such a reaction is understandable because the instability caused by uncertainty can be immediately disruptive. It's understandable, but it is also a mistake. Sometimes the survival of an organization depends on its ability to quickly adapt. Adaptability is learned, and for the organization to learn, there must be positive, forward-looking conversations, free of backward-looking accountability constraints. Chapter 11 specifically covers the after action review (AAR) process, a forward-looking, analytic meeting to ensure problems are being identified. It teaches leaders how to create a culture of candor, where no one is afraid to admit to a failure—and how to make the organization better as a result.
- **Chapter 12:** Uncertainty and crisis often create the conditions for failures to occur—individual, team, or organizational. Handling failures, large and small, especially during crisis and uncertainty, is a key element of effective leadership. Chapter 12 teaches how leaders may decide if a failure is worth letting people go or retaining them. It reveals how actual senior leaders made decisions to fire or retain people who made major mistakes. The emphasis is not on the mistakes themselves, but on how people react to those mistakes

following their occurrence. It covers the best responses for a person who has failed as well as the analyses made by leaders when deciding whether to retain that person. Anyone with the ability to fire or be fired—which is nearly everyone—will improve their abilities through Chapter 12.

- **Chapter 13:** This chapter describes how to handle the eventual medical dilemmas that we all will have in our lives. We use transplant diagnosis as the classic medical uncertainty and walk through a real-world example of how transplants work. Because of the need to suppress immune systems to retain transplanted organs, there is no end to the uncertainty of transplants. All of us will eventually face devastating medical diagnoses for ourselves, our family members, or both. We don't like to anticipate it, but it is true. This is an extraordinarily important chapter.
- **Chapter 14:** This chapter recognizes that in uncertain times or crises, leaders can be criticized, undercut, and otherwise targeted by others. We describe it as a political attack, and we mean business interpersonal—not national or local political matters. The chapter helps leaders recognize when such negativity is forming and lays out various strategies for defending oneself from those who may be taking you down.
- **Chapter 15**: This chapter orients us to the future, how to take the many practices described in the book and apply them. It specifically looks at the performance of a superior business leader in a major crisis and takes us all forward.

The book also contains two appendixes that cover the biographies of outstanding leaders that we interviewed and the interview questions they were asked, as well as exercises and reflection prompts to add to the practical application of leadership.

Need for Courage in Leading Through Crisis and Uncertainty?

We have seen books, TED Talks, leadership presentations, and other activities centered on the need for courage in leadership. People seem to love to talk about courage. It is such a positive quality when shown by those who display it. There are unlimited inspirational stories about courageous leaders. It sells. But realistically, a focus on courage does not directly account for what commonly causes leaders to fall short.

We take a different view. Rather than focusing our courage, we would simply say, "don't engage in cowardice." That's an unusual and somewhat dramatic statement. Seldom do people discuss cowardice, or what it is, or how it impacts leadership. Let's unpack this, and as a first point, know that we never label anyone as a coward. In our view, it's not the quality of an individual. But people—all of us—can act in ways that would be defined as cowardly. How so?

A key element of many dictionary definitions of cowardice includes behavior reflecting **excessive self-interest**. Consider a trite, symbolic example of cowardice, where a soldier flees from a fight, leaving his comrades behind. A soldier fleeing is not simply because they are fearful; everyone feels fear in combat, everyone. Along with fear, someone must exude excessive self-interest to leave others in the fight. In business, government, nonprofits, all organizations, people work with some degree of self-interest, that's completely normal. It negatively impacts both leadership and followership, however, when self-interest becomes excessive. It is far less important for leaders to be courageous than it is for them to simply *not* perform with excessive self-interest—in other words, to behave cowardly. Excessive self-interest is common in business and politics. For leaders to not be excessively self-interested is important, but it does not really require courage. Good leaders put their people first. Period.

After reading through these chapters, each of which gives you a challenge to use them in your organization, you are likely to have some concerns about trying them for the first time. Each of the chapters provides plenty of detail and guidance for you to successfully execute the techniques.

We have felt that same concern. Here is our advice: just do it. After you have executed the techniques once or twice, you will experience the benefits. Does it take courage? As the authors, one a combat veteran and one currently living in an invaded country's war zone, we would say, no, save your courage for something much more significant! It's your job! Just do it.

PART

I

Understanding the Crucible

It rarely begins with drama. It begins on a normal morning—the kind where leaders open laptops, check overnight e-mails, scan dashboards, and sip their habitual coffee. At 9 a.m., the metrics make sense. At 9:07 a.m., they don't. A missile lands near the office, communications go dark, and employees try to reach loved ones amid sirens. A new virus has been detected. A geopolitical conflict is escalating. A cyberattack spreads silently through global servers. A new AI model is released that threatens to upend an entire industry overnight. Something shifts. And in the span of minutes or hours, the predictable world quietly dissolves.

Leaders across the world remember their "day everything changed"—a moment when the assumptions they had built their strategies on suddenly felt naïve. In Ukraine, that day was

February 24, 2022, when cities woke to explosions, and entire workforces scattered. Plans crafted over months evaporated in a single headline. This is the threshold moment when leadership transitions from managing complexity to navigating uncertainty.

The old world rewarded those who planned well. The new world rewards those who can learn, adapt, interpret, and respond before the world settles into its next shape. Especially when the "new shape" is literally wartime chaos, with no functioning infrastructure or clear rules.

This prologue opens the door to that world—a world where clarity matters more than control, where resilience replaces certainty, and where leadership is forged not in stability but in disruption.

CHAPTER

1

The Nature of Uncertainty

A decade ago, many leaders still believed in predictability. Strategies were drawn up for five or even ten years ahead; industries moved at a measured pace; global trends were observable and, with the right foresight, manageable. But somewhere between digital transformation, the pandemic, and geopolitical upheaval, the illusion cracked.

For Ukrainian leaders in 2022, this illusion shattered overnight: offices bombed, teams evacuated, critical services disrupted. Predictive models meant nothing; immediate human decisions were all that mattered.

Today, events unfold faster than leadership hierarchies can process. A social media post can wipe billions off a company's valuation overnight. A new technology can rewrite the rules of an entire sector before an annual strategy review even takes place. A missile strike can destroy a data center before plans for redundancy can be executed. For leaders, this is not the exception—it has become the rhythm of modern life.

This chapter explores the forces that make our world so unpredictable, the difference between uncertainty we *can* manage and the kind that defies preparation, and why the leaders of tomorrow will not be defined by how tightly they control—but by how clearly they communicate.

Forces Shaping a Volatile World

When people speak about "uncertainty," it can sound abstract—like fog on the horizon. But for leaders, it's not fog; it's the landscape itself. The volatility we face today doesn't come from one direction. It's the product of overlapping, amplifying forces that interact in unpredictable ways.

Technological Disruption

Artificial intelligence (AI), automation, and platform-based ecosystems are rewriting entire industries. The half-life of skills is shrinking. The boundaries between human and machine work blur more each year. For every new opportunity—personalized medicine, intelligent logistics, creative automation—new risks emerge: cybersecurity breaches, ethical dilemmas, reskilling challenges.

In war zones, these challenges are compounded: AI may help optimize evacuation routes, but power grids and communications may already be disabled. Leaders must integrate tech with crisis improvisation.

The most adaptive leaders now see technology not as a wave to ride but as weather to navigate—uncontrollable, shifting, but predictable in its unpredictability.

Global Interconnectedness

In an interconnected world, a ripple in one region can become a shockwave in another. A shipping disruption in the Red Sea can delay production in Poland and retail in Chicago. A virus outbreak in one city can ground flights across continents within hours.

When Ukraine's logistics and IT systems were disrupted by war, ripple effects impacted global supply chains, international clients, and partner ecosystems instantly.

Interdependence has made our economies efficient—and fragile. Systems optimized for speed and cost often collapse under surprise. As one CEO put it during the pandemic, "Our just-in-time model worked beautifully until 'just in time' became 'too late.'"

Societal Shifts

Employees, customers, and citizens are asking different questions now. What does this company stand for? How does it treat its people? What's its contribution beyond profit? In a war, "what you stand for" becomes literal: commitment to employee safety, national solidarity, and ethical decision-making under fire.

Sustainability, inclusion, flexibility, transparency—these aren't nice-to-haves anymore. They're expectations. And when expectations shift faster than structures, leaders find themselves navigating not just operational uncertainty, but moral and cultural uncertainty too.

Environmental and Health Crises

Climate change has moved from a distant concern to a lived experience. Floods, wildfires, and pandemics remind us how easily human systems are disrupted by forces of nature. War adds another layer: infrastructure destruction, displacement, and trauma amplify environmental and health crises. The past few years have shown how fragile our "normal" truly is—and how much resilience depends not on prediction, but on preparation.

Political and Economic Instability

Trade wars, inflation, shifting alliances—each adds another layer of unpredictability. Even stable markets now move like tides, not clockwork.

During conflict, political instability is immediate: foreign diplomacy, sanctions, supply chain collapses, and emergency regulations. Leaders operate under rapidly changing legal and operational constraints.

Together, these forces create a world where *no one can control everything—but everyone must learn to navigate it.*

The Essence of Leadership in Uncertainty

The landscape of uncertainty is shaped by forces beyond any single leader's control, yet it is precisely in navigating these forces that leadership is tested. Understanding the difference between what can be anticipated and what must be confronted in the moment is the first step toward leading effectively under volatility.

Predictable vs. Unpredictable Uncertainty

Not all uncertainty is equal. Some types you can foresee; others arrive like lightning.

Predictable uncertainty follows patterns. Economic downturns after market bubbles, technological shifts as new innovations mature—these can be anticipated, even if not precisely timed. Scenario planning, diversification, and strategic agility can help organizations prepare.

Unpredictable uncertainty—a "black swan" event—comes without warning. A sudden invasion, a pandemic, a viral technology breakthrough like generative AI. You can't forecast these moments. What you *can* do is build systems and cultures that can adapt when they happen.

Many leaders burn energy trying to control the uncontrollable—micromanaging risk instead of equipping people to act under ambiguity. But control is a false comfort. The true art of modern leadership lies in distinguishing between what can be predicted and what must simply be faced.

In wartime, the line blurs dramatically: missile strikes are entirely unpredictable, while partial evacuation protocols may be planned. Leaders must constantly distinguish between what they can anticipate and what must be acted upon with courage in the moment.

Why Clarity Matters More Than Control

For much of the twentieth century, leadership was synonymous with control. Plans were made at the top; performance was monitored at the bottom. The assumption was that stability came from order.

But in the twenty-first century, order often collapses under its own weight. The tighter the system, the more brittle it becomes. The moment something unexpected happens, control-based leadership freezes—waiting for instructions that never come.

In war, control is an illusion: communications fail, power grids go down, transportation is blocked. Leaders' only leverage is clarity—guiding teams with purpose, transparent information, and defined priorities.

What replaces control is *clarity.* Clarity of purpose: everyone understands the "why" behind actions. Clarity of priorities: teams know what matters most right now. Clarity of roles: people know who owns what—even when plans change.

When clarity replaces control, teams can act quickly without waiting for permission. Leaders stop pretending to have all the answers and instead create the conditions for rapid learning.

Amy Edmondson, who coined the term *psychological safety*, often says, "The leader's job isn't to know everything—it's to make it safe to learn everything." In uncertain times, that is the essence of clarity (Edmondson, 1999).

Cultivating Shared Understanding

As we step back from the whirlwind of forces shaping our world—technological acceleration, geopolitical shifts, social transformation—a single truth emerges: Uncertainty is not a temporary storm to outlast. It's the permanent climate of modern leadership.

The challenge is not to restore predictability but to redefine leadership within unpredictability. The best leaders today act as sense-makers rather than controllers. They interpret complexity, give meaning to chaos, and help others find direction amid noise.

Clarity becomes their tool for resilience. When a team understands *why* it exists and *what truly matters*, it can move with confidence even as the path ahead keeps shifting.

Leadership in this new era is less about commanding outcomes and more about cultivating shared understanding. It's about guiding people through ambiguity with honesty and composure—offering them not false certainty, but steady clarity.

Mini-case Studies: The Nature of Uncertainty

Let's look at two mini-case studies to illustrate the points in this chapter.

Mini-case 1: Leadership in the Fog of War

In the early hours of February 24, 2022, when Russia launched its full-scale invasion of Ukraine, the country's business landscape changed in an instant. Offices in Kyiv, Kharkiv, and Mariupol were shelled. Employees woke up to explosions. Entire teams fled with only hours' notice. Mobile networks and internet connections were unstable. What had been a normal workweek became a national emergency.

Ukrainian companies—from IT firms like SoftServe, N-iX, and EPAM Ukraine, to logistics giants like Nova Post, to retailers like Rozetka—suddenly operated in extreme uncertainty. No one knew what the next hour would bring, let alone the next quarter (Nova Post, 2022).

Leadership Challenge Executives, line managers, team leads, and HR directors faced the ultimate test of decision-making under ambiguity:

- How do we protect people spread across dozens of cities?
- How do we communicate when networks fail?
- How do we sustain operations when the external world is collapsing?
- And most importantly—how do we give clarity when we ourselves have none?

This was uncertainty in its rawest form: no data, no forecasts, no control.

Actions Taken Despite the chaos, Ukrainian leaders moved with remarkable speed and clarity of intent. Across industries, several patterns emerged.

Immediately Prioritizing Safety Companies like N-iX and Intellias activated emergency protocols within hours:

- Established relocation assistance hotlines
- Arranged buses and cars to move employees and families westward
- Provided shelters, temporary housing, and psychological support
- Coordinated with city authorities and volunteer networks

Safety was not a statement—it was an operational decision.

Rapidly Creating Communication Lifelines With normal channels unreliable, leaders built redundancy:

- 24/7 crisis Slack/Telegram groups
- Daily video briefings
- SMS fallback chains
- Client updates every few hours
- Clear guidelines on who to contact in emergencies

Even when leaders didn't have answers, they shared what they did know and committed to updating employees the moment anything changed.

Being Radically Transparent with Employees and Clients Executives openly shared

- what risks the company faced,
- what parts of the business might be paused,
- what financial projections looked like, and
- what decisions were being made and why.

Transparency reduced fear—people fear silence more than bad news.

Redefining Roles and Priorities Companies quickly distinguished

- mission-critical operations,
- stabilization tasks, and
- nonessential work to pause.

Teams were empowered to make decisions on the ground when central coordination wasn't possible.

Outcome Against every prediction, many Ukrainian companies remained fully operational—sometimes within 48–72 hours of the invasion. Tech firms like SoftServe and N-iX kept client delivery uninterrupted (SoftServe, 2022). Nova Post restored service routes before some government agencies did. Rozetka resumed e-commerce deliveries in active war zones within weeks. Employees consistently reported one thing: "We trusted our leaders because they told us the truth." The companies that communicated openly and prioritized clarity built extraordinary loyalty—and in many cases, grew stronger culture than before the war.

Lesson When the world becomes unknowable, clarity becomes a lifeline. Ukrainian leaders could not control the war, but they could create pockets of certainty—through communication, prioritization, and grounded decision-making. In extreme uncertainty, clarity is not a luxury. It is the only form of leadership people can hold onto.

Mini-case 2: OpenAI and the Acceleration Shock: Navigating Hyperspeed Innovation

In 2022–2024, the rapid evolution of generative AI transformed global industries faster than any previous technology cycle. Companies that had barely adopted cloud computing suddenly faced AI systems capable of writing code, generating designs, automating workflows, and reshaping entire business models. OpenAI, a company with a few hundred employees, triggered global shifts affecting millions of workers and billions in market value—within months rather than years.

Enterprises accustomed to long strategy cycles found themselves unprepared for the speed of change. Leaders reported that traditional planning models were breaking down: by the time a strategy was approved, the underlying assumptions were already outdated.

Leadership Challenge How do leaders make decisions when the technological landscape evolves faster than their organizations can process? The challenge wasn't merely understanding AI—it was accepting a world in which clarity existed only moment-to-moment, and the future had to be navigated without stable predictions.

Actions Taken Organizations that responded effectively demonstrated a shared pattern:

- **Adopting rapid learning cycles:** Weekly AI task forces replaced annual strategy retreats.
- **Empowering cross-functional experimentation:** Teams tested AI tools directly rather than waiting for top-down directives.
- **Focusing on principles, not predictions:** "Responsible adoption," "human oversight," and "fast prototyping" replaced long-term roadmaps.
- **Investing in employee upskilling:** Companies like Accenture and PwC launched massive AI training programs, building internal clarity even as the external environment shifted (Accenture & PwC, 2022–2024).

Outcome Companies willing to embrace ambiguity and experiment early gained competitive advantage: faster development cycles, cost reductions, and new service offerings. Those who hesitated found themselves reacting to competitors rather than shaping their own direction.

Lesson In the age of exponential technology, clarity doesn't come from prediction—it comes from adaptability. Leaders who accept uncertainty as the new normal move faster and learn faster than those who wait for stability that will never return.

Exercise: Mapping Uncertainty in Your Organization

Take a blank sheet of paper. Draw two columns; label one "Controllable/Partly Controllable" and the other "Not Controllable."

Now, list all major sources of uncertainty affecting your organization—market volatility, client demands, technology shifts, supply chain risks, talent retention, regulatory changes.

Discuss the following with your team:

- Where do we focus planning and prevention?
- Where do we focus on adaptability, communication, and learning?

It's a deceptively simple exercise but one that reframes how leadership energy is spent: away from impossible control and toward intelligent clarity.

Leadership Reflection

Uncertainty is not the enemy of leadership—it is its truest test. The question is never, "Can I control this?" It is, "Can I bring clarity when no one else can?"

Nassim Nicholas Taleb uses the term *antifragile* to describe systems that grow stronger under stress (Taleb, 2012). Not resilient—*stronger*. A resilient system resists shock. An antifragile one learns from it.

Leadership in uncertainty mirrors this concept. The goal is not to preserve the old structure but to *use disruption as data*. Organizations become antifragile when leaders focus on clarity of purpose, rapid feedback loops, distributed decision-making, and experimentation rather than perfection. Clarity, not control, becomes the source of adaptability.

If uncertainty is the climate leaders must operate in, *crises are the storms that test the vessel itself*. Some storms destroy. Some storms reveal strength that wasn't visible before. The next chapter explores how leaders are transformed—sometimes permanently—by the crucible of crisis.

CHAPTER

2

Crisis as the Leadership Crucible

Every leader, at some point, meets the moment when the world stops following the rules. Markets crash overnight. A product flaw spirals into a public scandal. A war erupts. The routines and plans that once defined competence suddenly become irrelevant. These are the crucible moments—the fires that test who a leader truly is. The term *crucible* comes from metallurgy: a vessel where intense heat melts metal so its impurities rise to the surface. What emerges from the process is something purer, stronger, and more resilient than before.

Leadership crucibles work the same way. They are the moments of extreme pressure that strip away pretense and reveal essence. In the heat of crisis, decisions are made not from theory but from values. People look at the leader and ask—sometimes silently, sometimes aloud—"Can I trust you to get us through this?"

These moments can break a leader or make them. They can destroy reputation or forge character. Yet, almost always, they transform.

In wartime, crucible moments are immediate and existential. Leaders in Ukraine, for example, had to make life-or-death operational decisions under fire: moving civilians, protecting staff, restoring power grids, and maintaining communications. The speed of escalation is unmatched: crises can unfold minute-to-minute instead of days or weeks, testing both cognitive and emotional resilience simultaneously.

Why Crises Expose Leadership Truths

Crises are truth machines. They strip away hierarchy and expose the fragile difference between authority and trust. In ordinary times, systems and structures can mask weaknesses. Clear policies, predictable workflows, and familiar habits hold everything together. But when those structures collapse, what's left is the human element—courage, empathy, and clarity.

People don't look to leaders for perfection in crisis; they look for *presence*. They want someone who can hold the fear without spreading it, interpret chaos into meaning, and make decisions when no option feels safe.

Crises have a way of amplifying both strengths and flaws:

- The empathetic leader becomes the team's anchor.
- The visionary becomes the strategist others rally around.
- But the micromanager becomes paralyzed, and the ego-driven leader isolates themselves.

As Harvard's Ronald Heifetz observed, "Leadership is not about answers; it's about mobilizing people to face reality"

(Heifetz et al., 2009). And reality in crisis is always uncomfortable. That's what makes it transformative.

War exposes gaps in preparation instantly. Ukrainian leaders saw that hierarchies and protocols designed for "normal" operations became irrelevant under missile attacks and city evacuations. Trust, courage, and clarity replaced bureaucratic authority as the primary stabilizing factors.

Moments That Shape Leadership Identity

Leadership identity isn't formed in conference rooms; it's forged in moments of uncertainty. A CEO navigating a financial collapse learns what transparency really costs—and why it's worth it. A hospital director during a pandemic discovers that resilience doesn't come from control but from community. A startup founder, facing layoffs, finds the courage to admit fear without losing credibility.

These are crucible moments—not because of the scale of crisis, but because of the *internal shift* they provoke. A crisis forces leaders to action:

- Decide with incomplete information.
- Balance speed with compassion.
- Communicate when they don't have all the answers.

Every such experience leaves a mark. Some scars become wisdom. Over time, these trials shape a kind of quiet confidence—not the confidence of certainty, but of *capacity*: the knowledge that "I can stand the heat and still think clearly."

Leadership identity forms under immediate threat to human life. Decisions in wartime have irreversible consequences; hesitation can mean casualties. Leaders must operate under extreme moral and ethical uncertainty: prioritizing lives, balancing mission-critical operations with humanitarian responsibility.

Turning Pressure into Strength

What determines whether a leader breaks or grows under pressure? It often comes down to three stabilizing anchors: mindset, values, and relationships.

- **Mindset:** The ability to see a crisis not as catastrophe but as a curriculum. Leaders with a growth mindset ask, "What is this teaching me?" rather than "Why is this happening to me?"
- **Values:** When the noise of crisis drowns out logic, values become the compass. Leaders who act from deeply held principles—fairness, integrity, care—maintain coherence when everything else fractures.
- **Relationships:** No one leads alone through chaos. The strength of trust built before a crisis determines the speed of recovery during it. As one Ukrainian business leader said in 2022, "The first week of the war showed us that trust was our only real infrastructure."

Crises don't just test systems; they test the invisible glue of leadership—how deeply people believe in you, your word, and your purpose.

Mini-case Studies: Crisis as the Leadership Crucible

Let's look at two mini-case studies to illustrate the points in this chapter.

Mini-case 1: Leadership Under Fire in Ukraine: Clarity and Courage in Wartime

When the full-scale invasion began on February 24, 2022, Ukrainian leaders in every sector—energy, logistics, education, tech, government, humanitarian organizations—were thrust into what can only be described as a leadership crucible. Nothing in their experience prepared them for what unfolded in those first hours:

- Major cities under missile attack
- Teams scattered across the country
- Infrastructure damaged or destroyed
- Airports closed, borders jammed
- Parents trying to evacuate families while still holding responsibility for their teams

Within a single morning, every familiar system collapsed. This was not just uncertainty—it was existential shock.

Companies such as DTEK (energy), Ukrenergo (power grid operator), and Ukrzaliznytsia (railways), and organizations like the Lviv IT Cluster faced immediate decisions that carried real consequences for human lives.

Leadership Challenge The crisis stripped leadership down to its fundamentals. It was no longer about strategy or vision or quarterly plans. The questions became painfully simple:

- How do we keep our people alive?
- How do we communicate when networks fail?
- How do we make decisions when every hour rewrites the scenario?
- How do we lead when we ourselves are afraid?

In this crucible, titles mattered far less than courage, clarity, and human connection.

Actions Taken Across sectors, leaders responded with extraordinary decisiveness and humanity. Several patterns emerged that defined wartime leadership.

Setting Clear Priorities When Everything Else Was Chaos Organizations like Ukrzaliznytsia made an immediate shift: evacuating civilians, rerouting trains under bombardment, repurposing commercial operations for rescue missions.

The priority hierarchy was simple and unwavering: **people first → critical operations second → everything else later.** This clarity saved countless lives and prevented paralyzing confusion.

Communicating Continuously and Transparently Leaders at DTEK, Ukrenergo, and various regional IT associations held daily—sometimes hourly—updates with employees, partners, and communities. Even when information was incomplete, they shared what they knew, what they did not know, what they were doing next, and where to find help.

Uncertainty was everywhere, but silence was nowhere. Leaders discovered that **honesty is stabilizing**, even when the message is, "We're still assessing."

Empowering Local and Frontline Decision-making Traditional hierarchies disintegrated under war conditions. At Ukrenergo, engineers restoring power after missile strikes often had minutes—not hours—to make decisions. Central offices couldn't coordinate every action, so leadership shifted decisively: authority moved to where information lived—on the ground. This empowerment allowed teams to act fast, improvise solutions, and maintain essential operations despite constant threats.

Pairing Courage with Humanity At the Lviv IT Cluster, leaders organized shelters, relocation buses, humanitarian hubs, and medical support for thousands of employees and families. Managers were not just decision-makers—they became caregivers, coordinators, and human anchors. People remember not only the instructions they received, but the tone they were given in: steady, compassionate, and present.

Outcome What could have been organizational collapse instead became a story of resilience and unity.

- Ukrzaliznytsia executed one of the largest civilian evacuation operations in Europe since WWII.
- Ukrenergo kept the national grid functioning despite continuous missile attacks—an engineering and organizational miracle.
- IT organizations across the country relocated tens of thousands of employees, maintained client delivery, and even onboarded new business within weeks.
- Trust within teams deepened to a level many leaders say they had never experienced before.

Employees look back on those months not as the end of stability but as the moment their organizations **discovered who they truly were.**

Lesson Crises reveal the core of leadership. They burn away pretense, expose values, and demand a level of clarity, courage, and humanity that everyday life rarely requires. In the crucible of war, Ukrainian leaders learned a timeless truth: **control is a myth—but clarity, courage, and trust endure**. It is not titles that hold organizations together in crisis; it is leaders who stay grounded when the world falls apart.

Mini-case 2: Microsoft's Cultural Rebirth Under Satya Nadella

By 2013, Microsoft was widely seen as a declining giant. Internal teams competed instead of collaborating. Innovation had stalled. The company had missed mobile, cloud was slipping away to Amazon, and its once-dominant brand felt outdated. Employees described the culture as "rigid," "politicized," and "afraid of mistakes." For many insiders, the crisis was existential (Microsoft, 2014–2020).

Leadership Crucible When Satya Nadella became CEO in 2014, he stepped into a culture in turmoil. The crisis he inherited wasn't a market event; it was internal—a decades-long erosion of trust, psychological safety, and shared purpose. His crucible was not to save a product. It was to save a culture.

Actions Taken

- **Publicly acknowledging the cultural crisis:** Saying things like, "Renewing our culture is the most important thing I will do as CEO."
- **Replacing a "know-it-all" culture with a growth mindset:** Inspired by the work of Carol Dweck (2006).
- **Shifting from internal competition to collaboration-first values:** Breaking down silos and redesigning incentives to reward shared success over individual wins, fostering cross-team collaboration, knowledge sharing, and collective accountability for outcomes.

- **Simplifying the strategy around a clear purpose:** "Empower every person and organization to achieve more."
- **Modeling vulnerability and empathy:** These were qualities in big-tech leadership at the time.
- **Making bold strategic calls:** This signaled a shift from control to partnership. Examples include open-sourcing. NET and acquiring LinkedIn.

Outcome Microsoft regained momentum, rebuilt trust internally, and reemerged as one of the world's most valuable companies. But more importantly—it rediscovered its identity. Employees describe Nadella's leadership as "the moment the company grew up" (Nadella, 2017).

Lesson Crisis doesn't always come as an external shock. Sometimes it is cultural stagnation, fear, or loss of purpose. The crucible that transforms a leader—and an organization—can be the courage to name what is broken and rebuild from the inside out.

Exercise: Learning from Leadership Under Pressure

Think of one leader you admire for how they handled a crisis—in business, government, or your own experience. Ask yourself:

- What qualities made them effective when pressure was highest?
- How did they communicate or decide differently from others?
- What emotions did they manage—both their own and their team's?

Write down three lessons you could apply in your own leadership role. Then, consider this: What "crucible" might you already be in without naming it as one?

Leadership Reflection

Crises don't create leaders; they reveal them. They peel back layers of control and habit until what's left is the leader's core. Those who emerge stronger aren't necessarily the boldest or most strategic—they're the ones who stay grounded in purpose while holding others steady in uncertainty.

As Warren Bennis, who popularized the "leadership crucible" concept, once wrote: "The most dangerous leadership myth is that leaders are born. The truth is that leaders are made—and usually made in the crucible of experience" (Bennis, 2009).

Every crisis, no matter how painful, holds a choice: to harden, to break, or to transform. The heat is unavoidable. What you become through it—that's the art of leadership.

Psychologist Robert Kegan later described a similar phenomenon in adult development: crises push leaders from managing complexity to *transforming how they make meaning*. A crisis challenges the following: assumptions, ego, worldview, emotional resilience (Kegan & Lahey, 2009). Leaders who grow through it develop a deeper form of wisdom—the ability to interpret chaos, not just survive it.

But even the strongest leader can freeze or falter when emotions surge. A crisis does not just disrupt systems—it disrupts the human mind. To lead others through chaos, leaders must first understand the psychological terrain of uncertainty. The next chapter turns inward.

CHAPTER

3

The Psychology of Leading in Chaos

Uncertainty doesn't just shake economies or disrupt strategies—it shakes people. When the world becomes unpredictable, our first battle isn't out there in the market or the battlefield; it's inside our own minds.

The brain is designed for patterns, for cause and effect. It likes to know what's coming next. But in a crisis, that pattern disappears. Ambiguity feels dangerous, and our nervous system responds as if we're facing a physical threat. Heart rates rise, judgment narrows, and urgency replaces reflection.

For leaders, this is treacherous territory. They face the same fear as everyone else—yet they are expected to be calm in the storm. In these moments, leadership becomes not just a cognitive skill but an emotional discipline.

This chapter explores how uncertainty reshapes human thinking, why emotional intelligence becomes essential for leaders in turbulent times, and how to create psychological safety when fear runs high.

In war, uncertainty triggers **acute stress responses**: hypervigilance, narrowed attention, and rapid decision-making under fear of injury or death. Leaders experience simultaneous personal and organizational threats: their homes and families are at risk while they must command others.

How Uncertainty Affects Human Behavior

Behavioral science has long shown that uncertainty is one of the most powerful psychological stressors. The brain interprets it as a loss of control—and control is deeply tied to our sense of safety.

Neuroscientist David Rock (2009) describes this as a "status threat": when people can't predict outcomes, they experience it almost like pain. The prefrontal cortex—the part responsible for reasoning and planning—goes offline, while the amygdala, our internal alarm system, takes over. The result? We think less and react more.

Common patterns emerge repeatedly in moments of chaos:

- **Fear:** Imagining worst-case scenarios, losing confidence, second-guessing every move
- **Denial:** Clinging to the hope that the storm will pass without change
- **Urgency bias:** Acting just to *do something*, even when waiting or reflecting would lead to a better decision

During the early weeks of the COVID-19 pandemic, psychologists noticed a global rise in "urgency decisions": companies made hasty announcements, individuals panic-bought goods, and governments rushed to declare measures that later needed correction. The human need to *feel* in control can often override the need to *be* effective.

In extreme crisis, like war, fear responses are amplified: Ukrainian leaders reported rapid panic among teams during early missile attacks. Denial is dangerous: ignoring threats in wartime can be fatal, unlike in corporate crises where losses are mostly financial. Urgency bias can be life-threatening: acting too quickly without situational awareness can endanger staff or civilians.

Leaders are not immune to these impulses. But unlike most people, their reactions ripple outward—shaping how entire teams think and behave.

The Leader's Emotional Balancing Act

In crisis, every word, facial expression, and silence of a leader carries meaning. Teams read cues constantly: *Is the boss calm? Is she afraid? Should I be afraid too?* That's why leadership in chaos is not about suppressing emotion but about mastering it.

Leaders who overreact spread panic. Leaders who withdraw create confusion. But leaders who acknowledge their emotions, then center themselves before communicating, model the very steadiness others need.

A 2020 McKinsey study found that during uncertainty, employees' trust rose most not from optimistic messages but from *authentic presence*: leaders admitting, "We don't know exactly what's next, but here's what we're doing right now." That mix of honesty and action signals strength (McKinsey & Company, 2020–2021).

Think of New Zealand's Prime Minister Jacinda Ardern during the first pandemic lockdown. Her live briefings combined facts with empathy; she spoke as both head of state and fellow human. That emotional transparency didn't weaken authority—it reinforced it (Ardern, 2020).

A leader's emotions are the weather system of the organization. Calm leadership creates visibility; turbulent leadership clouds judgment.

Creating Clarity in the Fog of Chaos

When uncertainty peaks, people crave three things from those they follow:

- **Simplicity**. Complex plans overload anxious minds. Simple, consistent messages cut through noise and give direction.
- **Acknowledgment**. Pretending "everything's fine" insults reality. Naming fears helps people process them and move forward.
- **Psychological safety**. Teams think more clearly and act more creatively when they know mistakes won't lead to humiliation or punishment.

Amy Edmondson, who coined the term *psychological safety*, found that high-performing teams are not those with fewer mistakes but those that talk about mistakes openly. In chaos, this principle becomes vital: fear shuts down innovation faster than any lack of skill.

In war, clarity includes actionable, life-preserving guidance: evacuation routes, shelter availability, and critical mission priorities. Psychological safety is literal: employees need to trust that following guidance will keep them alive.

Creating psychological safety doesn't erase fear from external events—it replaces inner paralysis with collective courage. It's what lets teams experiment when the rulebook no longer applies.

Mini-case Studies: The Psychology of Leading in Chaos

Let's look at two mini-case studies to illustrate the points in this chapter.

Mini-case 1: Staying Calm Under Fire: Emotional Resilience in Wartime Ukraine

When Russia launched its full-scale invasion in February 2022, millions of Ukrainians woke to explosions, evacuations, and the shattering realization that nothing familiar could be relied upon. For leaders—in tech companies, telecom providers, media organizations, and volunteer networks—the psychological shock was immediate and overwhelming. At Kyivstar, employees struggled to keep communication services running while worrying about their families. At MacPaw, teams were scattered across shelters, basements, and border crossings. At Ukrainska Pravda, journalists were working under constant threat while documenting the unfolding national trauma. Volunteer organizations like Nova Ukraine and grassroots crisis-coordination groups were flooded with requests from people desperate for help. In this environment, leaders were not only managers—they were emotional anchors. But they themselves were scared.

Leadership Challenge How do you lead with emotional steadiness when your own home may be under fire? How do you make decisions when uncertainty triggers panic? How do you support your team when you are grieving, exhausted, or in shock? The core challenge was psychological: **how do you regulate your own fear so that you don't amplify the fear around you?**

Actions Taken Across organizations, leaders began practicing a form of real-time emotional leadership—grounded, human, and radically honest.

- **Naming the Fear—Not Hiding It:** Instead of projecting stoic denial, many leaders made a different choice: **acknowledge emotions openly.** Executives at MacPaw told their teams: "Everyone is scared. Us too. We're not pretending this is normal." At Kyivstar, managers began daily calls by checking in on people, not projects. Naming the fear helped reduce its power.
- **Clear, Short, Frequent Updates to Combat Rumors:** During the first weeks, misinformation spread faster than facts. To counter the psychological chaos, leaders shared: short morning updates ("Here's what we know today"), evening summaries ("Here's what changed"), safety advisories, availability of shelters, transport, or humanitarian resources. Even "We don't know yet; we will update you tomorrow" created emotional stability. The predictability of communication became a calming ritual.
- **Creating Safe Emotional Spaces:** Companies and volunteer groups established: virtual "check-in" rooms, team-specific well-being channels, mental-health drop-in sessions, managers trained in psychological first aid. In one Kyiv-based design firm, the entire team gathered for a five-minute "emotional roll call" each morning. This simple act helped people feel less alone.
- **Modeling Grounded Decision-making:** Leaders practiced a principle often repeated during those weeks: **"Slow is smooth, smooth is fast."** This mantra prevented decisions made from panic. For example, at media organizations, editors slowed down publishing processes to avoid mistakes

driven by adrenaline, in volunteer networks, coordinators paused shipments to double-check safety routes instead of rushing evacuations through dangerous zones. Emotional regulation became an operational skill.

Outcome Despite the trauma, teams across Ukraine reported something unexpected: they felt calmer and more connected than before the war. Employees said:

- "My manager made me feel safe even when nothing was safe."
- "What helped most wasn't information—it was their calm tone."
- "I learned what real leadership looks like."

Psychological safety—often treated as a "soft" cultural idea—became the backbone of functioning during a crisis. It allowed teams to think, communicate, and collaborate, even under missile attacks, displacement, or the uncertainty of each new day.

Lesson Emotional intelligence is not optional in chaos—it is structural. Leaders who acknowledge fear, regulate their own emotions, and create safe psychological environments help their teams navigate the unthinkable. In Ukraine's darkest hours, emotional clarity became as essential as operational planning.

Mini-case 2: Slack: Leading Through Psychological Overload

When COVID-19 forced millions of employees into remote work almost overnight, Slack shifted from a productivity tool to global infrastructure. Teams were isolated, anxious, and overwhelmed with messages. Inside Slack, employees faced extreme workload spikes, emotional exhaustion, and fear about the future.

Leadership Challenge Slack's CEO Stewart Butterfield recognized that the real threat wasn't technical failure—it was **psychological overload**. He had to guide teams facing chronic stress, blurred work–life boundaries, continuous digital interruptions, and uncertainty about customers, revenue, and personal well-being (Butterfield & Sutton, 2020–2021).

Actions Taken Butterfield's leadership became a case study in emotional intelligence under collective crisis:

- **Modeling Vulnerability Publicly:** Admitting he was struggling too, normalizing emotional honesty
- **Reducing Cognitive Load:** Inside the company by removing nonessential meetings and creating no-meeting blocks
- **Encouraging Psychological Decompression:** Through flexible schedules, mental health days, and permission to "log off without guilt"
- **Communicating Transparently:** About business risks, performance, and expectations so teams didn't spiral into catastrophic thinking
- **Shifting Product Features:** To reduce user overwhelm—threading, better notifications, asynchronous tools—showing empathy for customer stress

Outcome Slack became both a tool and a psychological support system for millions. Internally, employees reported higher trust in leadership despite burnout risks. The company maintained stability, continued innovation, and ultimately was acquired by Salesforce at a valuation of $27.7 billion.

Lesson In modern crises, emotional overload is a business risk. Leaders who recognize and address the psychology of chaos create the conditions for clear thinking and sustainable performance.

Exercise: Reframing Your Stress Triggers

Every leader has personal triggers—the things that spike anxiety or cause reactive decisions. Identify one that affects you most: perhaps sudden changes, incomplete data, or high-stakes presentations. Then ask:

- What story am I telling myself about this situation?
- Is there another way to see it that keeps me grounded?

For example, instead of thinking, "I must have all the answers," try, "My role is to create clarity and invite others into problem-solving." Instead of "Everything depends on me," reframe to "The team's strength is our shared adaptability."

Write down one reframe you can practice the next time stress takes over. Awareness is the first act of leadership under pressure.

Leadership Reflection

Uncertainty scrambles the mind long before it breaks the system. It triggers fear, urgency, and denial—the enemies of wise decision-making. The leaders who navigate it well aren't those who suppress emotions, but those who understand and direct them. Self-awareness, empathy, and emotional regulation become the core tools of command. And when leaders cultivate psychological safety, they give teams what the world cannot: a sense of stability amid chaos.

Daniel Goleman's (1998) emotional intelligence model argues that self-awareness and self-regulation are the foundation of effective leadership. Amy Edmondson's research on psychological safety complements this: teams think more clearly when they feel safe to speak, question, and experiment. Together, they form the psychological architecture of effective crisis leadership.

At its heart, this architecture is built on four capacities:

- Understand your emotions.
- Regulate your reactions.
- Create safety for others.
- Encourage thinking under pressure.

Calm leadership is not personality; it is a trained practice. It is the discipline of choosing responses rather than being ruled by reactions. As Viktor Frankl (2006) wrote from his own crucible, "Between stimulus and response there is a space. In that space is our power to choose our response."

Leadership, at its psychological core, is the art of using that space—to breathe, to think, and to guide others toward clarity when everything else feels uncertain.

Uncertainty tests perception. Crisis tests courage. Chaos tests emotional discipline. Together, they form the crucible of modern leadership—a place where pressure doesn't just challenge leaders but reveals what they are truly made of. In these moments, leadership stops being a role and becomes a way of being.

When the familiar map dissolves, leaders discover that the real battlefield is internal. The noise, the fear, the urgency—all of it first unfolds within the mind long before it manifests in the world outside. What distinguishes steady leadership is not immunity to fear, but intimacy with it. Calm leaders do not deny their emotions; they learn to *interpret* them, to sit with discomfort long enough to see what others rush past.

From the experiences explored across these chapters, one truth becomes clear: **leadership is not the ability to control the environment, but the ability to remain grounded and purposeful within it.** Control belongs to stable times. Clarity belongs to uncertain ones.

The crucible teaches leaders to

- **interpret shifting conditions**, even when patterns are faint and incomplete;
- **act under imperfect information**, balancing intuition with evidence;
- **stay human while making hard decisions**, refusing to let crisis turn them into machines;
- **transform fear into clarity**, letting emotion inform, not dominate; and
- **build trust when stability collapses**, knowing trust becomes the currency of survival.

This inner transformation is not dramatic or loud. More often, it happens in quiet moments: the breath before addressing a panicked team, the pause before sending a message that will set the tone for hundreds, the decision to listen instead of reacting impulsively.

Calm leadership is not a personality trait. It is a practice—a discipline forged through repeated encounters with uncertainty. It is the ability to metabolize pressure, to convert tension into focus, and ambiguity into thoughtful action.

The leaders who thrive in turbulence are not those who attempt to outrun uncertainty, but those who learn to move with it. They understand that disruption is not an interruption of leadership—it *is* leadership. These leaders turn pressure into insight and disruption into direction. They embody the paradox of modern leadership: the steadier they remain inside, the more capable they become of shepherding others through the storm.

Part II builds on this foundation—shifting from understanding the nature of the crucible to cultivating the mindsets that allow leaders not only to survive uncertainty, but to lead brilliantly within it.

PART

II

Mindsets for Effective Leadership

Every leader remembers a moment when the world seemed to tilt—a moment when the playbook they trusted simply stopped working. Sometimes it happens slowly: a market that once felt predictable begins to churn, customer expectations shift, technology accelerates faster than anyone can learn it. Sometimes it happens in a single day: a phone call, a headline, a crisis that breaks open the illusion of stability. Leaders often describe this moment the same way: "It felt like the floor opened beneath me." The feeling is universal—but what happens next is not.

Some leaders freeze, waiting for the world to return to what it was. Others try harder to control the uncontrollable, tightening their grip until decisions become bottlenecked and teams grow anxious. And then there are those who lean into the uncertainty with a different kind of posture—not with helplessness, not with bravado, but with adaptability, curiosity, and calm determination. These leaders don't ask, "When will things go back to normal?" They ask, "Who do I need to become to lead in the world as it is now?"

Part II of this book is about that shift—the internal transformation that separates reactive leadership from adaptive leadership. It is the inner work that allows leaders to move from fear to clarity, from rigidity to resilience, from control to possibility. If Part I described the crucible, Part II describes what kind of leader emerges from it.

CHAPTER

4

The Leadership Mindset Shift

There is a moment in every crisis when leaders realize that the strategy is no longer the strategy and the plan is no longer the plan. This realization is unsettling—but it's also liberating. It marks the point where leadership stops being about managing circumstances and becomes about shaping responses.

In wartime Ukraine, this realization could occur within hours, as supply chains, workplaces, and people's safety shifted unpredictably. Leaders had to act before information fully formed, with consequences that were often operational and existential simultaneously.

In uncertain times, the decisive factor is not the leader's technical knowledge, nor the precision of their forecasts, nor the stability of their systems. It is their mindset—the lens through which they interpret events, make decisions, and influence others.

The right mindset doesn't remove uncertainty, but it determines whether uncertainty becomes a constraint or an opening.

During conflict, mindset is literally the operational system: clarity, composure, and adaptability allow teams to respond without losing cohesion under extreme threat.

This chapter explores the internal shift leaders must make to be effective in volatile environments: from seeking control to cultivating adaptability, from fearing disruption to learning from it, from clinging to old identities to evolving into new forms of leadership.

The Myth of Control in an Uncertain World

For most of modern history, leadership rewarded control. The best leaders were believed to be the ones who had the answers, anticipated risks, enforced order, and offered stability. But this model belonged to a world where change moved in linear, predictable patterns.

Today, complexity moves faster than control can keep up. Psychologists call this *the control paradox*: the more leaders cling to control in a dynamic environment, the less control they actually have. Control becomes a trap. It slows decisions. It suffocates initiative. It prevents the rapid learning needed to adapt.

Leaders who try to tighten every bolt in a crisis often find that their teams become passive, waiting for instructions that never arrive fast enough. Worse, the leader becomes overwhelmed—because the volume of information, emotion, and pressure is too much for any one person to handle.

The modern world doesn't reward perfect plans. It rewards adaptive intelligence. And adaptive intelligence begins with a shift in mindset.

From Control to Adaptability

The leaders who thrive in uncertainty share a common ability: they adapt faster than their environment changes. Adaptability is not improvisation. It's not chaos. It's a disciplined willingness to respond to reality instead of defending the past. Adaptable leaders do three things consistently:

- **They name reality without dramatizing it.** People don't need perfection from leaders—they need orientation. In a crisis, saying, "Here is what we know, here is what we don't, and here is what we're doing next," builds more trust than any illusion of certainty.
- **They learn faster than they judge.** Rigid leaders filter new information through old assumptions. Adaptive leaders update assumptions as quickly as new information emerges. In war, assumptions can change by the hour: a production facility threatened by shelling or a road suddenly blocked by conflict requires rapid updates and flexible responses. A 2022 MIT study found that companies with "high learning velocity" outperformed competitors during crises by up to 5×—not because they had better data, but because they processed it more openly (MIT Sloan Management Review, 2022).
- **They empower decision-making at the edges.** When environments move fast, local decisions become more valuable than top-down mandates. In this sense, adaptability is not only an individual mindset—it is a leadership choice about how power flows in a crisis.

The Three Inner Capacities of the Adaptive Leader

Adaptability is visible on the outside, but it begins with three internal capacities:

- **Resilience—absorbing shock without losing shape.** Resilience is not endurance. It is recovery—the ability to return to clarity after disruption. Resilient leaders respond, reflect, recalibrate. For Ukrainian leaders, resilience was tested not only by operational disruption but by the psychological toll of employees' safety and family welfare. Returning to clarity often meant balancing strategic decisions with life-critical considerations.
- **Courage—acting without complete information.** Courage is not the absence of fear; it is acting through fear. Crises often require decisions made in the gray zone, where the cost of waiting is greater than the cost of being imperfect.
- **Optimism—seeing possibility where others see threat.** Optimism is not positivity. It is perspective. It is the capacity to believe that actions matter, that teams can grow, and that crisis contains seeds of transformation. Research shows that leaders who pair realism with optimism are rated as twice as trustworthy, especially in turbulent times.

When Mindset Becomes the Message

Leadership is contagious. Not the words—the mindset behind the words. Teams take cues from how leaders interpret events:

- A leader who panics creates panic.
- A leader who blames creates fear.
- A leader who freezes creates paralysis.
- A leader who adapts creates possibility.

In wartime, a leader's composure is a signal of survival: panic spreads faster than logistical failure. Employees look to leaders for cues on how to act under threat.

A study from the Center for Creative Leadership found that during crisis, 70% of team behavior patterns mirrored the leader's emotional stance. That's why mindset is more than a personal preference—it is an organizational signal. In this sense, mindset becomes culture.

Mini-case Studies: The Leadership Mindset Shift

These two mini-cases illustrate how leaders confronted extreme uncertainty—one in the immediacy of war, the other amid a global pandemic—and how mindset shifts enabled effective action under pressure.

Mini-case 1: Leadership Mindset in Wartime Ukraine: From Control to Resilience

When the full-scale invasion began in 2022, many Ukrainian companies found themselves operating in conditions that made traditional management immediately obsolete. At Ajax Systems, a security-tech manufacturer, production facilities in Kyiv were threatened by active fighting. At Ukrposhta, the national postal service routes were cut off, drivers were sheltering, and depots were located in cities under missile fire. Teams at Grammarly and Reface were scattered across time zones within 24 hours. Leaders at Naftogaz and Beetroot faced the impossible: keeping critical services and operations running while their own employees were evacuating families or hiding in basements. The familiar structure of work—plans, approvals, deadlines, forecasts—disintegrated overnight (Ajax Systems et al., 2022).

Leadership Challenge The question leaders confronted was not "What is our strategy?" but "How do we lead when the situation changes faster than we can process it?" They could not rely on six-month plans, static organizational charts, or formal communication chains. People needed direction, but leaders were navigating the same fear, displacement, and uncertainty as their teams. This became a mindset crucible: control was impossible, but clarity, adaptability, and grounded leadership were essential.

Actions Taken What differentiated effective leadership was not resources or preparedness—it was the speed at which leaders abandoned control and embraced adaptability.

- **Radical Clarity Instead of Perfect Answers.** At **Ajax Systems**, executives began each day with a two-minute update: what was known, what was unknown, what decisions were made in the last 12 hours. No promises. No false certainty. Just grounded clarity.
- **"Safety First" as an Operational Principle.** Ukrposhta's CEO Ihor Smilianskyi ordered teams to preserve life above all. Deliveries resumed only when teams confirmed local routes were safe. This mindset prevented panic-based decisions and reinforced trust.
- **Fast, Iterative Decisions Instead of Long Plans.** At **Reface**, product and staffing decisions were made in small increments—hours or days, not weeks. The rule became: *"Make the best decision with the information you have. Adjust when reality changes."* This prevented paralysis and kept momentum.
- **Decentralized Action: Decision-making Moves to the Edges.** In Naftogaz's regional offices, engineers restoring

gas supply made autonomous operational calls because headquarters couldn't coordinate minute-by-minute. Leaders shifted from asking, "Why did you decide?" to "What do you need next?" This mindset unlocked speed and resilience.

- **Adaptive Operations: Build What the Moment Requires.** Several organizations created wartime workflows: backup communication channels in case of blackouts, twice-daily check-ins replacing weekly meetings, relocation task forces, cross-functional emergency teams, simplified approval chains. At **Beetroot**, the entire HR and Ops function reorganized within 72 hours around evacuation, resource allocation, and rapid client communication. This wasn't a plan—it was an adaptation made operational.

Outcome Because leaders shifted mindset quickly, many organizations remained functional—even productive—under extreme pressure. **Ajax Systems** relocated parts of its manufacturing and continued operations within days. **Grammarly** moved fully remote effortlessly, sustaining global momentum and customer trust. **Ukrposhta** restored mail routes in regions where utilities were still offline, becoming a symbol of national resilience. **Naftogaz** kept critical energy services running despite constant operational disruptions. **Beetroot** stabilized teams across multiple countries, strengthened client partnerships, and even expanded operations. Employees reported feeling informed, protected, empowered, and united. The crisis accelerated innovations that might have taken years in peacetime: remote-first cultures, decentralized decision-making, faster feedback cycles, clearer communication habits, more resilient operational structures. Many leaders later said: "This was the moment we discovered what we were truly capable of."

Lesson Wartime Ukraine showed—vividly—that leaders do not succeed by trying to **control** chaos. They succeed by changing how they **think**: from rigidity → adaptability, from perfection → clarity, from authority → trust, from fear → courage, from centralized control → empowered teams. The mindset shift is not theoretical. It is practical, operational, and immediately visible in behavior. When the world becomes unrecognizable, a leader's mindset becomes the most important system in the entire organization.

Mini-case 2: Reinvention at the Edge; Airbnb's Pandemic Pivot: Finding Opportunity in Collapse

In early 2020, as COVID-19 swept across the globe, travel came to a standstill. Borders closed, flights were canceled, and cities entered lockdown. Airbnb—a company built entirely on the movement of people—saw its bookings evaporate almost overnight (Airbnb, 2020). Within weeks, the company lost nearly 80% of its revenue, forcing mass cancellations, refunds, and a painful restructuring. Investors predicted bankruptcy. Some analysts suggested Airbnb's entire business model might be obsolete in a world defined by immobility and fear. It was a crisis without precedent—a direct strike at the core of the company's identity.

Leadership Challenge Airbnb's leaders faced a defining question: How do you lead when your entire industry collapses? No one could predict how long lockdowns would last or whether travel would ever return to pre-pandemic levels. The company did not have the luxury of waiting for clarity. The challenge required a radical mental shift: instead of clinging to the world that had existed, they needed to imagine the world that might emerge.

Actions Taken Rather than responding with panic or denial, Airbnb's leadership embraced a mindset of curiosity and reinvention. They reframed their crisis around three guiding questions:

- What needs are emerging in this new world? People still needed safe places to stay—but closer to home, for longer periods, and away from dense urban centers.
- What long-term behaviors might be changing permanently? The rise of remote work meant people could "live anywhere," not just vacation occasionally.
- What part of Airbnb's DNA remains relevant? A global community of hosts, personalized experiences, and a sense of belonging.

From these insights, Airbnb reshaped its entire strategy:

- Shifting from short-term tourist stays to longer-term rural and suburban stays
- Leaning into the rise of digital nomadism and remote-work travel
- Redesigning the platform to highlight "unique stays," cabins, countryside homes, and nature-based listings
- Strengthening support for hosts, many of whom relied on Airbnb income for survival
- Cutting unnecessary complexity and returning to core values: connection, simplicity, and trust

This was not a defensive retreat—it was a complete reimagining of what the company could be.

Outcome Within a year, Airbnb moved from near collapse to becoming one of the largest IPOs in tech history. Bookings in rural areas exceeded pre-pandemic levels. Long-term stays

(28+ days) became one of the fastest growing categories. Hosts expanded offerings; new communities joined the platform; customer behaviors aligned with Airbnb's redesigned model.

The company emerged leaner, more focused, and more aligned with the future of travel—not the past. What looked like an existential threat became the catalyst for the company's next chapter of growth.

Lesson Airbnb's story demonstrates a powerful truth about leadership mindset: opportunity often hides inside the heart of disruption. Leaders who see only risk become paralyzed. Leaders who combine realism with curiosity discover openings long before stability returns. Crises expose vulnerabilities—but they also reveal unmet needs, emerging behaviors, and strategic possibilities that would have been invisible in ordinary times. The organizations that innovate fastest under pressure are the ones whose leaders consciously shift from control to exploration, from fear to insight, from survival to reinvention.

Exercise: Practicing Adaptive Leadership

In the next month, identify three situations where you can visibly demonstrate adaptability to your team. For each one, write the following:

- **The situation:** What uncertainty or challenge might arise?
- **Your adaptive response:** What flexible behavior or mindset will you model?
- **The intended impact:** How will this help build trust, clarity, or initiative in your team?

Examples might include these:

- Sharing incomplete information with transparency
- Delegating a decision rather than centralizing it
- Adjusting a plan publicly and framing it as learning
- Changing your stance based on new evidence
- Asking for input instead of issuing a directive

Adaptability grows through practice—not theory.

Leadership Reflection

Every leader is shaped by the world they face—but leaders also shape the world by the mindset they bring to it. The internal shift from control to adaptability is not a technique; it is a transformation in identity.

Adaptive leaders learn to release the illusion that stability is something they create. Instead, they create clarity, trust, and learning—the only true anchors in turbulent environments.

The mindset shift is subtle yet profound:

- From rigid expertise to continuous learning
- From self-protection to courage
- From fear-driven reactions to grounded responses
- From managing tasks to empowering people
- From resisting change to evolving with it

In conflict, the alignment of mindset and human-centered actions becomes not only a cultural or strategic advantage but a mechanism for survival and continuity.

The leaders who thrive in uncertainty do not wait for conditions to calm. They step forward with openness, humility, and resolve. They embody the belief that leadership is not about certainty it is about direction. In this sense, mindset is the real compass.

If mindset shapes how leaders respond to crisis, then relationships shape how people respond to the leader. The next chapter turns the lens outward—to the human side of leadership—exploring why empathy, trust, and authenticity become powerful stabilizers when the world around us feels insecure.

CHAPTER

5

The Human Side of Crisis

Leadership in a crisis is often measured in decisions made, plans executed, and risks mitigated. Yet, the most lasting impact is rarely operational—it is human. In war, these decisions include life-and-death considerations: operational choices are inseparable from the human experience, and leaders' emotional stance directly affects morale and survival. Research in emotional intelligence demonstrates that the way leaders make people feel, seen, and heard determines whether a team survives turmoil or thrives through it (Goleman, 1998). Facts and figures may matter in boardrooms, but what people remember is how leaders made them feel when the world was unstable.

In times of upheaval, fear, confusion, and fatigue spread faster than any business risk. Teams facing rapid changes can feel disoriented, anxious, and isolated. Edmondson (2018) shows that when leaders respond only with directives and operational updates, psychological safety declines, and engagement drops. In contrast, leaders who engage with empathy, authenticity, and vulnerability create anchors of trust and clarity, allowing teams to navigate uncertainty with resilience, cohesion, and courage.

This chapter examines why the human side of leadership is critical during crisis and explores how leaders can model behaviors that foster trust, connection, and engagement. It shows how empathy, authenticity, and vulnerability are not signs of weakness, but strategic tools that define adaptive leadership. We will explore how leaders communicate, make difficult decisions, and balance human needs with business imperatives—and illustrate these points through vivid real-world examples.

Why Human-centered Leadership Matters Most in a Crisis

During crises, traditional metrics and business tools are not enough. Teams respond first to **human signals**, not operational directives. For Ukrainian organizations, simply ensuring staff knew which areas were safe or whether essential routes were operational was a critical human signal as well as operational necessity. When leaders acknowledge uncertainty, show concern for well-being, and act transparently, they build psychological safety, which allows teams to stay focused, take initiative, and innovate under pressure (Edmondson, 2018; Riggio & Tan, 2013).

Human-centered leadership works because it addresses two fundamental needs:

- **Orientation:** People need clarity about what is happening and what it means for them (Center for Creative Leadership, 2020).
- **Connection:** People need to feel recognized, cared for, and included in the response (Goleman, 1998; Brown, 2018).

Leaders who cultivate these dimensions ensure that trust and engagement remain intact, even under extreme stress. Human-centered leadership is not an add-on to operational leadership—it is integral to effective crisis management.

Core Dimensions of Human-centered Leadership

Empathy, authenticity, and vulnerability are core dimensions of human-centered leadership.

Empathy: Understanding and Responding to Human Needs

Empathy is the ability to perceive and respond to the emotions, needs, and experiences of others. In a crisis, empathy allows leaders to recognize the human impact of operational decisions, adapt communication to the audience's emotional state, and support teams in managing stress, uncertainty, and fear (Riggio & Tan, 2013).

Empathy is not about solving every personal problem—it is about acknowledging reality and demonstrating care. Teams who feel understood are more likely to stay engaged, collaborate, and trust leadership decisions (Goleman, 1998).

Empathy in war extends beyond work stress; it involves acknowledging mortal danger, displacement, and psychological strain, and actively mitigating them where possible.

Authenticity: Honesty and Credibility in Leadership

Authenticity means being truthful about challenges, limitations, and expectations while maintaining confidence in the path forward (Kernis & Goldman, 2006). It builds credibility because teams can trust that leaders are not hiding information or creating illusions of certainty. Authentic leaders

- communicate both the knowns and unknowns,
- admit when they lack answers, and
- model consistent behavior aligned with values.

Authenticity provides a stable reference point for teams in chaotic environments. It transforms anxiety into orientation and confusion into trust.

Failing to be authentic in such war conditions could create fatal confusion. Sharing uncertainty honestly, while providing direction, became an operational imperative.

Vulnerability: Relatability and Shared Humanity

Vulnerability is the conscious choice to show one's human side, admitting uncertainty or personal struggle (Brown, 2018). Leaders who embrace vulnerability become relatable rather than distant authority figures, foster psychological safety by normalizing discussion of fears and challenges, and encourage innovation and initiative by modeling adaptive courage.

Vulnerability signals trust in the team and invites reciprocal openness, strengthening cohesion under pressure (Edmondson, 2018).

In war context. showing personal concern or admitting one's own fear signaled safety to employees; it allowed teams to act confidently under threat rather than freeze.

Building Trust in High-pressure Times

During a crisis, trust is earned through clarity and care, demonstrated consistently through behavior and communication. Key trust-building actions include the following:

- Regular updates that are candid, concise, and actionable
- Recognition of emotional strain alongside operational performance
- Two-way communication that encourages questions, feedback, and dialogue
- Demonstrating calm and measured responses under stress

Leaders who balance transparency and compassion preserve engagement, loyalty, and organizational stability, even when delivering difficult messages or implementing operational changes.

Crises often create tension between operational imperatives and human well-being. Tough decisions—such as layoffs, cost-cutting, or process restructuring—are unavoidable. What distinguishes effective leaders is how they execute and communicate these decisions (PwC, 2021).

Leaders who explain the rationale behind difficult choices, listen to team concerns without defensiveness, and treat people with dignity and fairness can maintain trust and engagement. In these moments, human-centered leadership becomes a strategic advantage—enabling operational goals to be met without sacrificing morale or loyalty.

Mini-case Studies: The Human Side of Crisis

These next mini-cases highlight how leaders maintained human connection, trust, and operational continuity under extreme and global disruptions, showing that leadership is as much about people as it is about process.

Mini-case 1. Leading with Humanity: Logistics and Essential Services in Wartime Ukraine

The 2022 invasion of Ukraine plunged the country into unprecedented disruption. Organizations providing essential service—transportation, logistics, and retail—were suddenly forced to operate under conditions that made standard management systems obsolete.

Ukrzaliznytsia, the national railway operator, faced the dual challenge of keeping freight lines and passenger services running while safeguarding employees whose homes and families were directly affected by conflict. Simultaneously, Epicentr K, a leading home goods and retail chain, had to maintain its supply chain, open stores where possible, and ensure delivery of essential items to communities, all while dealing with logistical obstacles, road closures, and staff displacement. Leaders at both organizations were not only grappling with operational chaos but also the emotional toll on their teams, many of whom were living in constant fear, taking shelter in basements, or evacuating family members.

Leadership Challenge Leaders confronted a stark reality: traditional top-down management could not function under these circumstances. Decisions had to be made faster than centralized approval systems could handle, and employees needed reassurance, clarity, and care. The challenge was to maintain operational continuity without sacrificing human well-being—a delicate balancing act where every choice carried immediate consequences.

Actions Taken The following actions were taken:

- **Radical Transparency:** Daily briefings were established at both organizations. Ukrzaliznytsia provided updates on which rail lines were operational, where trains could safely transport goods, and what contingency plans were in place. Epicentr K communicated openly about which stores could operate, anticipated delivery delays, and logistical constraints, emphasizing honesty about uncertainties rather than offering false certainty.
- **Prioritizing Human Safety:** Leaders placed employee safety above all else. Ukrzaliznytsia rerouted trains away from high-risk zones and set up emergency accommodations for staff working essential routes. Epicentr K introduced flexible shifts, temporary relocation support, and mental health counseling, acknowledging that employees' physical and emotional safety was paramount.
- **Empathy in Action:** Leaders held frequent one-on-one and group check-ins, asking not just about work but about personal well-being. Listening sessions allowed employees to voice fears and frustrations, while executives openly acknowledged the stress, sharing their own experiences of coping under uncertainty.
- **Empowering Teams Locally:** Authority was decentralized to allow regional managers and frontline supervisors to make real-time operational decisions. This included rerouting shipments, adjusting delivery priorities, and opening or closing stores as conditions dictated. Local teams felt trusted to respond to dynamic realities without waiting for headquarters' directives.
- **Adaptive Operations:** Both organizations rapidly restructured operational processes. Ukrzaliznytsia set up temporary coordination hubs and backup communication channels to

ensure essential freight and humanitarian aid could move. Epicentr K created micro-distribution centers closer to affected areas to sustain supply chains, and simplified approval processes allowed faster decision-making.

Outcome Despite active conflict, both Ukrzaliznytsia and Epicentr K maintained critical operations, delivering essential goods and transport services where possible. Employees reported feeling supported, empowered, and recognized, sustaining engagement even under extreme stress. Leaders observed a marked improvement in team autonomy and problem-solving, revealing a resilience and adaptability that had previously been latent. The crisis accelerated adoption of decentralized decision-making, rapid operational adjustment, and human-centered communication practices, forming a foundation for long-term organizational resilience.

Lesson Crisis leadership is not only about operational efficiency—it is fundamentally human-centered. Leaders who communicate openly, prioritize safety, listen empathetically, and empower teams can sustain trust, engagement, and performance, even in life-threatening circumstances. Organizations that maintain this balance are not only surviving—they are building new capabilities that strengthen them for the future.

Mini-case 2: Human-centered Leadership in a Temporary Global Crisis—IKEA Supply Chain Disruption 2020–2021

During 2020–2021, IKEA experienced a global supply chain disruption caused by port closures, factory shutdowns, and bottlenecks in international shipping. This affected manufacturing, warehouse operations, and retail availability worldwide.

The crisis threatened not only operational performance but also customer trust and employee morale, as teams faced increased workloads, uncertainty, and the stress of keeping operations running under unprecedented conditions.

Leadership Challenge How could IKEA continue to operate effectively, support employees, and maintain customer trust when supply chains were unstable and timelines unpredictable? Leaders needed to navigate operational pressures while demonstrating empathy, authenticity, and adaptability, ensuring employees did not feel abandoned or overburdened (IKEA Group Reports, 2020–2021).

Actions Taken The following actions were taken:

- **Transparent Communication:** IKEA leaders implemented multi-channel updates for both employees and customers. Staff received detailed information on inventory status, shipping delays, and operational priorities, while customers were kept informed about potential disruptions and alternatives. The message was clear: uncertainty existed, but it would be managed openly.
- **Empathy and Support:** Teams were working overtime under unusual conditions. Leadership introduced flexible schedules, mental health support, and acknowledgment of employee effort. Recognizing the human cost of disruption was as important as operational management.
- **Authenticity and Vulnerability:** Executives admitted that not all challenges could be fully controlled, sharing openly about supply constraints and potential delays. By modeling vulnerability, they fostered trust and encouraged employees to engage without fear of blame.

- **Empowering Teams Locally:** Store managers, warehouse supervisors, and supply chain coordinators were authorized to make real-time decisions on product prioritization, stock allocation, and local logistics solutions. This decentralization allowed rapid adaptation and reinforced a culture of trust.
- **Operational Adaptation:** IKEA established temporary regional supply hubs, diversified suppliers to reduce dependency on single sources, and reprioritized product flows to ensure high-demand items remained available. Internal processes were adjusted to reflect changing realities, balancing operational efficiency with employee capacity.

Outcome IKEA maintained operational continuity across regions despite severe supply disruptions. Employee engagement remained high, supported by empathetic leadership and clear communication. Customer trust was preserved, with transparent updates and proactive management of expectations. The organization gained long-lasting operational and cultural improvements, including increased flexibility, employee empowerment, and crisis-ready supply chain processes.

Lesson Even temporary crises highlight the importance of human-centered leadership. Transparent communication, empathy, authenticity, and local empowerment enable teams to remain engaged, adaptable, and resilient. Leaders who model care, honesty, and practical problem-solving create an environment where people can contribute effectively, even when uncertainty is high.

Exercise: Planning Human-centered Communication

Plan a communication to your team during uncertainty:

1. Identify the key facts your team needs to know.
2. Determine how you will demonstrate empathy—recognizing emotional strain, uncertainty, or fears.
3. Decide how to balance honesty and reassurance—showing confidence in the future without minimizing challenges.
4. Consider actions beyond words—meetings, check-ins, resources, and decision-making transparency.

Leadership Reflection

Crisis exposes the human dimension of leadership more clearly than any other situation. Leaders who cultivate empathy, authenticity, and vulnerability create anchors of stability that guide teams through uncertainty. These qualities are not abstract ideals; they are strategic capabilities, essential to sustaining engagement, trust, and performance.

The human side of crisis leadership rests on three pillars:

- **Empathy:** Recognizing and responding to the experiences and emotions of others
- **Authenticity:** Being truthful about challenges while modeling confidence and stability
- **Vulnerability:** Showing humanity and **admitting uncertainty to strengthen relatability**

When leaders consistently combine clarity, care, and connection, they achieve resilient, engaged, and innovative teams. They transform fear into motivation, confusion into orientation, and disruption into opportunity.

In practice, this means

- communicating honestly and frequently, even when answers are incomplete;
- treating team members with dignity, fairness, and respect;
- delegating and empowering others;
- modeling trust and adaptability; and
- providing resources and structures that address both human and operational needs

Human-centered leadership is a force multiplier. It sustains organizations through the immediate crisis and shapes culture long after the storm has passed. Teams remember how they were treated, and leaders who invest in these dimensions leave lasting impact—on people, performance, and the organization's ability to thrive in uncertainty.

Leadership is not measured by control or perfect execution—it is measured by how leaders guide, connect, and inspire people when the world is at its most unpredictable. In this sense, the human side of leadership is both the heart and the compass of adaptive organizations.

Having seen how mindset, clarity, and human-centered leadership anchor teams in crisis, we now shift to action: the practical techniques leaders can use immediately to guide, empower, and sustain performance under uncertainty.

PART

III

Specific Techniques for Leading in Uncertainty

Parts I and II of this book described, in detail, the effects of uncertainty and crisis on the needs of followers, which can then be met by the best of leaders. Ideally, you already have an improved understanding of the nature of uncertain and critical situations and an improved understanding of how things work in the worst of times.

Part III is a bit less about understanding and more about doing. Chapters 6 through 15 are designed to provide tools that engage and improve leadership. Each has independent value—they may be used one at a time, without interactions among them. They are designed to be immediately useful; you can apply them the moment you finish reading about them. Each technique has not only been written about, but each has been used repeatedly and effectively by one or both of us. They work.

CHAPTER

6

Creating Constructive Dialogue as a Leader

In this chapter, we will answer the question, "How can you be a stronger leader across the meetings we all have?"

Perhaps the single, most universally common interactions that leaders have with followers are meetings. For some leaders, meetings are a daily event. Tom, commanding a unit of 600+ soldiers in South Korea, had a daily meeting, at 5:30 a.m., with eight direct reports. The environment was considered "semi-combat," which means continued uncertainty of combat near a declared enemy force. The meetings continued for 26 months, during which there were more than 15 alerts driving the preparations for war. While that example is extreme, frequent meetings are still very common in business and politics. For example, we had a client who had three meetings a week, every week, with direct reports. Leaders have meetings with followers.

How Uncertainty Affects Meetings

The advent of a crisis and the pervasive fog of uncertainty fundamentally alter the nature and function of meetings. They transform from routine collaborative spaces into high-stakes arenas demanding decisive leadership, transparent communication, and a heightened awareness of the psychological toll on participants. Meetings during turbulent times are characterized by a pronounced shift in dynamics, a laser focus on immediate decision-making, and an urgent need to foster psychological safety amid heightened stress and anxiety.

The primary effect of uncertainty on meetings is a pivot toward a more centralized and directive style of leadership. The typical consultative and consensus-driven approach often gives way to a "command and control" model. This is born out of the necessity for swift, decisive action in the face of time sensitivity and incomplete information. Leaders are expected to provide a clear vision and a steady hand, guiding the team through the turmoil. This shift, however, necessitates a delicate balance. While decisiveness is crucial, it must be coupled with empathy and transparent communication to maintain trust and prevent the erosion of morale.

It is important not to overly simplify the preparation of meetings, or the control exerted during them, especially in uncertainty. Take, for example, the complexity that Judge Lina Hidalgo faces with meetings of the Harris County Commissioners Court:

> So, we have a law in Texas that prevents us from chatting about issues before the governing body outside of a public setting, and so uncertainties are at the heart of the meetings. We're only allowed to talk to one other colleague, and so I can't talk to, you know, colleague B, and have B talk to C. I mean, just each of us just gets one. And if, and if I've already talked to

> B, I can't talk to C. So, you know, it's been interesting in the sense of, like the principal versus staff. So, we were able to have meetings at the staff level.
>
> There are all sorts of steering committees to try to figure out, for example, there's one, there was one to figure out how to invest the billion dollars that we received from the Biden administration and covid recovery funds. And so proposals would come really exciting programs, from de letting homes to helping make sure that there's wireless internet all around the county to, you know, homelessness reduction, which we actually succeeded at, to early childhood education and so it was the steering committee's focus to evaluate the various proposals and, you know, choose the really good ones. But ultimately that had to come before the governing body, and we had to vote yes. And there was no guarantee that whatever the steering committee members do is what their principals are going to do at the Commissioners Court. So generally speaking, you know, we do follow what the staff has come up with, but not always.

It's easy to see the complexity and challenge of some meetings experienced by Judge Hidalgo and the leader responsibility for controlling them not merely with direct actions, but with flexibility, humility, and strategy.

Uncertainty, the insidious partner of any crisis, profoundly impacts the cognitive and emotional state of meeting participants. The lack of clear information and the multitude of potential negative outcomes can lead to "decision paralysis," where individuals and teams become frozen, unable to commit to a course of action for fear of making the wrong choice. This is often compounded by heightened stress and anxiety, which can impair rational thinking and lead to flawed decision-making. Research shows that under duress, individuals may resort to cognitive biases such as confirmation bias—favoring information that confirms preexisting beliefs—or wishful thinking, further jeopardizing the quality of decisions made in crisis meetings.

To counteract these psychological impacts, effective crisis meetings must prioritize the creation of a psychologically safe environment. This involves acknowledging the anxieties and uncertainties faced by the team. Leaders who are open about what they don't know and who encourage open dialogue without fear of reprisal can help alleviate some of the cognitive load on participants. This transparency builds trust and allows for a more realistic assessment of the situation.

Best Practices for Meetings

Mark Thompson, a top CEO coach, advises that uncertainty requires leaders to be courageous in entering meetings, because the direction of the meeting could be unpredictable:

> In business, to the extent that uncertainties are high, you're less likely to invest, and the required rate of return has to be higher. I think the same metaphor applies in meetings. How risky is it to have the courage of our convictions about naming the uncertainties and having the pre brief, the brief and the debrief?

The agenda and structure of meetings also undergo a significant transformation. Routine topics are often sidelined in favor of a singular focus on the crisis at hand. Emergency meetings become the norm, demanding immediate attention and a clear, urgent tone. Best practices for such meetings include the following:

- **Clear Purpose:** The meeting's objective must be explicitly stated from the outset, ensuring everyone understands the gravity of the situation and the required focus.

- **Designated Roles:** Assigning specific roles, such as a dedicated notetaker, frees up the leader to facilitate the discussion and decision-making process effectively.
- **Structured Brainstorming:** While the situation is urgent, a structured approach to brainstorming solutions is essential to avoid chaotic and unproductive discussions.
- **Clear Action Items and Accountability:** Every decision must be translated into a clear action item with a designated owner and a deadline. This ensures that the meeting translates into tangible progress.
- **Consistent Follow-up:** The initial crisis meeting is rarely the last. A regular cadence of follow-up meetings is crucial to track progress, adapt to new information, and maintain momentum.

In conclusion, crisis and uncertainty act as a crucible for meetings, stripping them down to their most essential functions: rapid decision-making, clear communication, and the reinforcement of shared purpose. They demand a more directive style of leadership, a heightened sensitivity to the psychological well-being of participants, and a rigorous, action-oriented approach to a transformed meeting agenda. The ability to effectively navigate these challenging dynamics can be the difference between successfully weathering a storm and succumbing to the chaos.

Town Halls

One type of meeting that is difficult for most involved leaders are "town hall" meetings—meetings with groups of 50–200, with open questioning to the leader. In the United States currently, town hall meetings with politicians are common and problematic. US Republican congressmen having town halls have lost the ability to control their meetings to the point where they have been advised by their political leadership to stop having them.

Some believe that it is because Democratic activists are deliberately disrupting them; others believe that it is concerned citizens expressing their anger. As is usually the case, both are likely true.

Lieutenant General Mark Hertling is descriptive about the need for control during meetings, with the example of the disrupted political town halls reflecting his approach:

> Disruptive meetings throw you off your plan, and no one likes to be thrown off their plan and (forced to) adapt. So, the reaction to someone doing that is basically you being in a not steady stance where you can address the things you want to address, and you have to shift the dynamic of your thought process to thinking on the fly, trying to figure out what comes next, and literally adapting to someone else. I mean, it causes you to not keep going at a steady state. So you have to figure out ways to best adapt, and there are ways to do that.

In addition to their use for politicians, town halls are also quite useful for academic and business leaders. In those circumstances, the best leaders find ways to control dialogue. Uncontrolled dialogue in open meetings is a recipe for disaster—as politicians have found out. It allows people with specific agendas—some well-meaning, some not—to take over the direction and purpose of the meeting. Competent leaders always put rules or procedures in place that give them some control over the dialogue. Such control must be done thoughtfully and carefully, so as not to give followers the impression that the meeting is somehow rigged. Town hall meetings are not effective unless participants feel that they can all be heard.

Card Stacks

One of the best ways to control dialogue in a meeting, yet all be heard, is what we call "card stack." To card stack a meeting, give each participant a blank card, 3 × 5 or 6 × 8. At the beginning of the meeting, ask them to write on one side something that the organization (or you the leader) is doing well. On the opposite side of the card, ask them to write something that the organization (or you the leader) is not doing well. Give them about three minutes, then collect up their answers to form a card stack. You now have tremendous power in your hand.

The nature of the card stack is that of a visible indication that everyone in the room has been given a chance to provide input. In the leader's hand, it represents the entire group. Once stacked, the leader may then start reading the cards, one at a time. As it's done, the response can be a leader's comment or explanation, or dialogue with the room. Do not automatically read both the front and back of a card. Start by reading two or three positive comments, then select a negative comment to respond to. Holding the card stack, the leader has the opportunity to balance out the positive and negative, and we recommend maintaining more positive comments than negative ones. Control the tone.

Often in crisis or uncertainty, negativity emerges in the meetings. In some cases, it's simply warranted because of threatening outcomes. In other cases, individuals may have their own agenda in being negative, and they may be persistently so. In such instances, the card stack is a terrific aid. The leader can address the negative issue to the right degree, then point out that the card stack is large and that the group can't focus too long on one single issue—an issue that could also be dealt with at a later time in a different context.

The card stack is an advantage, but it also represents a responsibility by the leader to respond to the written comments, not necessarily immediately in the meeting, but at some point soon after. If an issue has been written into the card stack, those who wrote it know that the leader knows. If the leader is viewed as responding over time, it's a hugely positive perception and will result in even more employee contributions in meetings. It's a huge liability, though, if people know that the leader is informed of issues that are not dealt with. It will result in less feedback and honesty, less confidence that the leader is effective, and less trust. The strength in results that could be either positive or negative is an indication of the power of this technique.

Other Tips

Bernard Banks is an academic leader who has a history of highly effective meetings, and he has specific thoughts about the impact of uncertainty in the ability to control effective meetings:

> The impact of uncertainty in meetings is that you have to create a very cognitive group process. Uncertainty can result in a variety of things, either starting to ask better questions or leaning into trying to create certainty when you're truly not certain, which can result in groupthink and a variety of other things. And so can you create an environment where people can actually hold that tension that exists because of uncertainty. And instead of saying, "We've got to rush to action right now," start to really refine, "Well, what are the questions that we really need to explore?" A lot of leaders value certainty because certainty allows them to take action. But I think the best ones force patience, to drive introspection, by really examining what are the questions that matter?

Banks continues:

> And I think that you know in combat, one of the things you learn when you've been shot at a lot, "slow is smooth, smooth is fast, and smooth is precise." The best leaders don't seek to speed things up. They seek to slow things down so you can respond in a more effective way. And I think in meetings, when uncertainty starts to creep in, can you resist that temptation to say, "Okay, well, let's, let's do something," as opposed to, "Okay, let's stop, assess, reflect, and then drive that into our decision-making cycle."

Meetings are absolutely crucial to leadership, and meetings in conditions of uncertainty are even more critical. Such meetings also require more thought and preparation—unlike the disrupted political town halls where leaders simply waited for questions to emerge and then tried to answer them, as criticisms and uncertainty rained down. Virtually all leaders should give more careful thought to the planning and management of meetings. They are far too valuable to set up poorly and allow to fail.

Better leadership in meetings will enhance your recognition of the knowledge that people hold, some of which could be the key to anticipating a crisis to emerge from uncertainty. The next chapter describes precisely how to create the expectation and recognition of an approaching disaster.

CHAPTER

7

Predicting When Your Organization Is Vulnerable

In this chapter, we will answer the question, "In the face of uncertainty, how can you best avoid falling victim to an unanticipated catastrophic event?"

One of the negative effects of uncertainty, crisis, and chaos is vulnerability to unpredicted catastrophic failures and unforeseen major problems. Without clear predictability, problems for leaders show up with little warning. This creates a worsening of the impact of whatever problem occurs because of lack of preparation, immediate disruption, and initially unclear solutions. Good leaders recognize this.

Alan Murray, when interviewed for this book, recognized the need:

> ... talk to lots of CEO and heard Julie Sweet, the CEO of Accenture, and in an interview I did at our London summit two weeks ago, I thought she put very well that in the time of such immense uncertainty, you can't predict, you can't forecast, you can't really even do planning, because so many things just don't show up in this area. So pandemic wasn't in anyone's scenario in 2019 and so what you really have to do is condition your team to deliver results in spite of the constant onslaught of unanticipated waves of disruption and change.

When hit with an unforeseen catastrophic problem, leaders are often presumed not to be at fault. The unexpected nature of the problem causes many to assume that the leader could not do anything before the problem arose. Sometimes that is true, but very often it is not. Most chaotic impacts have some degree of predictability. It is up to the leader to take action to uncover such threats, rather than simply responding reactively when they occur. How, then, shall a leader predict the "unpredictable"?

The best and most likely answer lies in the people being led, those who are most familiar with the organization's vulnerabilities. Think back to the last time you were in the midst of a major problem that erupted with little or no warning. In our experience, there is almost always a person off to the side, shaking their head, saying, "Well, I knew this was going to happen."

At that point, leaders often feel frustrated that the individual who thought that the problem was coming did nothing to warn or alarm the organization, or to prevent the problem for occurring. That indicates a leadership fault, not a fault of the individual. It could be that the individual was afraid to speak up, or that they were not completely certain of the issue, only suspecting it. The leader must set the conditions for those concerns to be overcome, so that they may assess the concern, and get ahead of otherwise unpredictable problems. A large percentage of unanticipated, catastrophic outcomes occur because of leader passivity.

The Problem with an Open Door Policy

How should a leader create the conditions for employee concerns to be revealed? One common attempt to stay approachable is the "open door policy," essentially an invitation for employees with issues to come in and speak to their leader. One of the authors led an organization of approximately 800 people and had a robust open-door policy that included not only his office, but welcomed access to his nearby home. It seemed almost impossible to be more transparent or accessible, and there was complete, honest commitment by the leader to be available. Leaving the organization after two years, the leader took a 360-degree assessment that looked at, among other things, perceptions of accessibility. He was surprised to find out that though both peers and superiors viewed him as highly accessible, at lower levels in the hierarchy, the perception was that accessibility was low. This was an important leader lesson about passive forms of availability. Simply put, they are ineffective, even when the leader is earnestly committed to accepting feedback, input, or observations. They also tend to stifle more active forms of feedback-seeking.

Open-door policies are passive. Despite its noble intentions, the open-door policy is fraught with potential challenges that can render it ineffective or even detrimental to an organization.

- **The Illusion of Openness:** Perhaps the most significant criticism is that an open-door policy can be a superficial gesture rather than a genuine commitment to open communication. If employees fear retaliation for speaking up, the policy becomes a hollow promise. A culture of fear will always trump a stated policy of openness.

- **Undermining Middle Management:** When employees consistently bypass their direct supervisors to air grievances with senior leaders, it can erode the authority and effectiveness of middle managers. This can create confusion in the chain of command and leave middle managers feeling disempowered and out of the loop.
- **Time Management and Productivity Drain:** For senior leaders, a constant stream of employee concerns, many of which could be handled by direct supervisors, can be a significant drain on their time and productivity. This can pull their focus away from strategic initiatives and turn their offices into a revolving door of complaints.
- **Lack of Anonymity and Fear of Reprisal:** Many sensitive issues, such as harassment or ethical breaches, are difficult for employees to raise directly with a named individual. The lack of an anonymous reporting channel can silence those who fear personal or professional repercussions.
- **Potential for Abuse:** The policy can be misused by employees who may use it to spread gossip, complain excessively, or attempt to gain favor with senior leadership. This can create a toxic environment and distract from legitimate concerns.

Conducting Pre-mortems

Rather than a passive approach to availability, an active approach is far more likely to gain participation by followers, and one of the best ways to pull out observations that may reveal an upcoming problem or issue. The most proven technique for this outcome is called a pre-mortem.

A pre-mortem eliminates the majority of issues with passive availability. The method of conducting a pre-mortem is as follows:

1. Assemble a group of knowledgeable employees representing all levels of the organization. Plan on about an hour-long meeting. Assemble a minimum of 10 people and a maximum of about 50 people.
2. Explain that the purpose of the meeting is to collect a series of catastrophic predictions, whether literal or imaginary.
3. Guarantee complete anonymity. Give each person a sheet of paper and a pen—nothing digital.
4. Ask the group, as individuals, to imagine a major fiasco affecting the organization, and to explain the failure. For example:

   "Our intent to achieve our organizations vision has failed because of an inconceivable turn of events. Six months have passed. We still exist as an organization, but with badly diminished potential. The opportunities that you once assumed would be created by working in our organization seem, at this point, out of reach. You are deeply concerned that our organization will no longer be a place where you can achieve your goals and become successful. The purpose of the organization is threatened. How could this have happened to us?" Prepare a list of reasons that might account for this outcome.
5. Remind them of their anonymity. Give them limited time to write, say, five minutes. Once they describe the fiascos and their effects on the organization, collect the papers.

6. At this point, begin reading the most interesting fiascos aloud, creating group discussions about threats to the organization. Some of the issues may be too sensitive to work on as a group, so those may be skipped—but understand that someone knows that you as the leader have seen what they have described.

Pre-mortems have other advantages. Dr. Gary Klein, a research psychologist, has looked at how repeated use of pre-mortems affects leader judgment (Klein, 2003). What he found is that the review of imaginary or potential fiascos improves a leader's intuition. The higher up in an organization a leader goes, the more important experience and intuition is rather than hard analysis. The greater the levels of uncertainty, and in crisis, the value of leader intuition skyrockets—at times being the only basis for decision-making.

Bernie Banks finds pre-mortems to be highly effective and is specific about aspects of managing them. In his words:

> I think pre-mortems are an excellent technique when utilized routinely, and that you can generally revisit your pre-mortems throughout a certain period of time, because most things have happened at least once in the world, and you can predict, if this thing was to transpire, what impact would it have on the operation, and what are ways in which we might mitigate the risk associated that in advance. So, somebody says, "We've never lost a nuclear power unit in our state," great. Well, a lot of folks would say, "Well, I spend time on that. It's, you know, proven energy source. It's great. It's fine. But you do, you should sit there say, if, in fact, we were to have a nuclear accident, what would impact be, and how would we respond to that? Even if somebody says, well, the likelihood of that occurring is not high, it's like that's not what we're talking about. We're talking about if, in fact, it did happen, How bad would it be, and is there anything we can do right now to lower the risk associated with it happening? Pre-mortems allow you to do that.

Also, note that although the request used in creating pre-mortems is for being creative and imagining fiascos, that real, potential problems are often revealed. Those with experience in the use of pre-mortems have found that the indirect approach of asking for imaginary input, rather than asking specifically, "What do you feel is a threat to us," is better able to get to possible problems. If one asks directly about threats, people often assume they need more proof that allows them to describe it.

As an example of the use of pre-mortems, an author's client, GE Power and Water, initiated use of pre-mortems. Two years later, they were asked for comments about the process, as well as permission to use them in leadership work. They said:

- "Good formal way to get the right people talking ahead of time. People know how to solve problems if they have time to do so. pre-mortems force that time and help prevent unnecessary fire-drills."
- "Great way to ensure smoother execution; have allowed us to achieve financial targets sooner in a few cases."
- "We sometimes use our Six Sigma tool—FMEA—to help facilitate the process. Simply, the FMEA asks what can go wrong, how severe could it be, rank orders the issues and develops action plans against the issues."

The Beneficial Results of Post-mortems

FMEA stands for Failure Modes and Effects Analysis. It's a process whereby an organization can list all the predictable problems and failures of a product, process, or event, and provide a solution for each problem. It is a very effective approach for managing rationally **predictable problems**. The advantage of the pre-mortem to the FMEA is that the pre-mortem has the potential to uncover irrational, otherwise unforeseeable problems as well.

One of Tom's first uses of pre-mortems was with a group of 40+ faculty members in an academic department. The process was directed at issues that could impact the department's effectiveness and reputation. One of the fiascos described an investigation of the department by the university leadership focused on class cancellations. The description of the fiasco cited a professor's last-minute cancellation of 11 classes in a semester. The issue was not highlighted to the entire group but was investigated internally. The discovery was not merely the cancellation of a large number of class sessions across several courses, but that the cancellations were being caused by a major drug and alcohol problem, significant enough to be a threat to the professor's life. The leadership was able to intervene, ensure that all classes were covered by capable individuals, and get help for the faculty member to gain better control over her addictions.

The department was saved from outside embarrassment, and the faculty member's career and life were likely saved by the intervention. Notably, it had been going on for months and never uncovered by an open-door policy or other passive means. Only by leader involvement in the active use of a pre-mortem did the issue emerge before becoming a major issue.

Judge Lina Hidalgo, the top executive in Houston's Harris County, is principally responsible for unpredicted disasters, floods, chemical fires, and major disasters. Her experience showed her that it's not only important to actively work to predict such disasters, but to assume that they are going to occur, and use formal or informal pre-mortems to create improved and effective preparedness:

> It's a balancing act, because there are only so many resources. There's only so much time, and there's always going to be things to do, and so it's a matter of assessing, you know, given the probability of this, given the impacts of this, and you know what the public sees as particularly important, Where does this issue fit? And does it make sense to invest time and dollars in preventing that particular catastrophic event, right? I guess it's, it's never going to be perfect in terms of, like, doing everything you could do to prepare, prevent and … be able to choose what we're going to do.

It is of course useful when a leader can pull the prediction of a catastrophe out of people who are retaining the information. The next chapter reveals how to create sufficient empowerment that people may rapidly take action themselves, for either eliminating a vulnerability or taking advantage of an opportunity.

CHAPTER 8

Fostering Initiative and Empowerment as a Leader

In this chapter, we will answer the question, "How can leaders create the conditions that enable people to take initiative, but the correct initiative, in fixing problems or achieving success?"

One highly important aspect of leadership is to foster initiative in followers, empowering them to have the trust and confidence to work without constant supervision and micromanagement. Uncertainty often gives leaders the feeling that greater control is necessary. The tendency is to become more "command and control," stifling the innovation and empowerment that leads to rapid solutions to problems. Uncertainty, as well as crisis, often puts followers in a position where they need to react quickly and independently in response to various outcomes.

Yet uncertainty and crisis diminish initiative and feelings of empowerment among employees. The result is a static, unresponsive organization that waits to be told what to do. Nothing could be more faulty than organizational paralysis at a time where quick responses could be the difference between success and failure as certainties emerge. Delegation should increase, not decrease. Here is Dr. Bernie Bank's take on increasing delegation in uncertain times:

> In uncertain times do I delegate more or less? I think the answer is it depends. It depends on where the uncertainty resides, who operates in that space, and what will it take for them to be able to operate effectively going forward? And so, if I'm already delegated to a large extent, and people feel as if they're equipped to act based on intent, understanding intent, and I don't need to delegate anymore. But if, in fact, where the uncertainty resides is that a higher level of action? I don't know, but I think the answer is, it depends. And I also think it depends on what's your what's your normal modus operandi? If you're already an organization that believes in empowering people down to the lowest levels and being an intent based organization, if you're an intent based organization, you already have created the conditions where people take actions and uncertainty because they understand the why. They understand what tasks have to be accomplished. They understand what success consists of. So, you don't really need to change how you're operating. But if you're more directive in your orientation, and now there are things transpiring that current directives don't actively address, then yes, you're going to have to change what you're doing.

Leaders should establish and maintain support to empowered employees taking initiative, in both crisis times and more normal circumstances. Alan Murray found a quote from one of his clients to be highly instructive:

To my last conversation, which was with a guy who was at FedEx for many years and now runs a company in Germany. He passed on, but here's the quote. He said, "Be stubborn on your vision, but flexible on your details." It's a two-part answer. You can't compromise on being the team going in the right direction, but you have to compromise under to define detailed responses that to you make sense. Okay, so I like that piece, in times of uncertainty, you have to be stubborn on your vision, but (flexible in how you manage).

Leader Intent Statements

Empowerment is being flexible in how you manage. It requires more than a leader's open mind, and hope that people take action. It requires a specific definition of both limits and opportunity for action. People generally do not take initiative unless they are confident that their actions will be supported by the leadership. It requires deliberate, active engagement of the leader. The best way to create such clarity is with a technique called *leader intent statement.*

Historically, leader intent statements were created by the US Army to provide supplemental guidance for plans. Plans initiated in uncertainty or crisis circumstances begin to decay the instant that they are released. The decay is so predictable that one of the classic quips is, "No plan survives first contact with the enemy," along with a similar emphasis, "Don't fight the plan, fight the fight." In business, competitor actions change. Available resources change. Baseline circumstances change. In the face of this, if the only guidance employees have is a degrading, increasingly ineffective plan, the tendency is to stop and wait for further guidance.

Leader intent statements defend against such stoppage. They create a set of boundaries that limit what could be the personal agenda of the employee and instead ensure that independent actions are aligned with the goals of the leader and the organization. Leader intent statements are composed of four types of information that trigger the ability for employees to act without further guidance. The four pieces of information are as follows:

1. **Purpose**. Leaders need to begin the intent statement by clarifying the purpose of the event, plan, operation, or other initiative. They need to explain the "why," and ideally, the explanation should take little more than a sentence.
2. **Methods and nonnegotiable tasks**. If there are specific methods that the leader wishes to be used, they should be stated here. It's not a requirement to be so direct, but if need be, this is the place to make it clear. This is also the place to specify any tasks that must be performed to the leader's satisfaction. Methods and tasks will be open to the employees if not specified here.
3. **Risk**. Often people limit their initiative because they fear retribution if things go wrong. This part of the intent statement is where leaders make clear what level of risk they are willing to accept and cover and what outcomes they do not want to occur. The covered risk could be a dollar amount, like $30,000, or $30,000,000, or in some instances, $0. It could refer to outcomes to be avoided, for example, "Do not risk the loss of a client." The risk references are to allow the leader to create limits but are also a form of clarity so that the empowered employee knows what they *can* risk. It gives them the ability to perform with confidence and little fear of reprisal. This section is also where the leader expresses anything they *do not* want to happen.
4. **End state**. It's very important for the leaders and those they lead to share an understanding of what the successful end

state will be. It represents a target of inspiration, a guide to shape all efforts in the direction of the intent. It keeps all on the same goal.

Those four pieces of information form a box of opportunity to take initiative, to move forward without detailed plans or guidance. There are some keys to the effectiveness of leader intent statements. In less than a page, guidance is given that can achieve the same amount of progress as a detailed, large-scale plan. The leader should minimize the guidance in the intent statement as much as they possibly can. If there is too much detail, too many tasks, it takes on both the form and the vulnerabilities of a plan. One of the authors reviewed the intent statement given along with the strategic plan for the US involvement in Afghanistan. Although the plans were hundreds of pages in length, the intent statement was less than a page and a half long. The intent statement was shared in the entire military hierarchy, with subordinate leaders writing their own intent statements that were within the boundaries of the intent statements written by leaders above them. It is very important and very helpful if intent statements are held and understood at all levels of the organization. It is the pragmatic embodiment of a common vision.

Case Studies

Tom initiated a large-scale project that serves here as an example of how intent statements can work independently of a plan. He was approached by a physician in Connecticut who had begun a series of summer plays, assisted by talented Broadway actors. The plays were at Sandy Hook, the location of a horrific mass school shooting in 2012 that killed 20 children between six and seven years old, and six adult staff members. The physician, a plastic surgeon named Michael Baroody, created a foundation named after the date of the shooting—the 12.14 Foundation—to support the student activities over the summer had asked our author if he could create a leadership development process internal to the play productions. Our author agreed, but after the doctor left, he realized he had neither the time nor the experience to put together a detailed plan, nor did he have the ability to use the people he supervised for this independent work.

In approximately an hour, he wrote an intent statement and emailed it to 40 leader development coaches and colleagues from Boston to Washington DC, asking them if they would like to participate in the initiative. Thirteen colleagues volunteered and assigned themselves portions of the project that aligned with their talents and experiences. The intent statement below is what guided all of their activity into a successful leader development activity for the organizer:

Intent for Development in the 12.14 Foundation Children's Summer 2014 Performing Arts Experience

(This statement provides broad guidance for volunteers and empowers anyone involved in the project to take initiative in line with the intent)

Purpose: Our purpose is to use our skills as leader development professionals to add value to the experiences of the children of Newtown who participate in the 12.14 summer performing arts activities.

Method (Key Tasks): Our approach may include, but is not limited to, the following:

- Building support, perhaps through a <u>coaching strategy</u> (group, peer, individual, or other).
- Building capability, perhaps through strategies to <u>enhance resilience</u> (confidence, self-efficacy, GRIT).
- Building agency, perhaps through learning to <u>give and receive feedback</u> (SBI or other framework).

Our methods will include the use of measures to estimate both the effectiveness of our interventions and the overall effectiveness of the 12.14 summer program as a constructive developmental experience. Our group will form into independent work teams where volunteers choose to work on Building Support, Building Capability, Building Agency, or another defined method, and deliver their professional services on the schedule of their choosing, coordinated centrally with our entire group and with the 12.14 creative director, Michael Unger.

Risk: We will limit the risk of unintended expansion of the project ("mission creep") by limiting student contact with each group to four hours over the summer (meaning that three proposed groups may engage students for 12 hours total, or a day and a half). Such a limit should shape the volunteer time investment to roughly four to six days over the course of the summer. This limitation is to protect both student time and volunteer time, and to discipline us to keep our interventions clearly defined, sharply focused, and crisply executed. We will limit the risk of legal exposure by making sure that we have parental consent for participation in our portion of the program and specifically, for any written or online assessments; we will not engage in one-on-one coaching, individual feedback, or other one-on-one activities. We will limit the risk of ethical breach by not engaging in any form of therapy (even if licensed to do so) and by avoiding the use of terms like "healing," "trauma," or "recovery," to avoid creating any false perceptions of our engaging in therapy.

End State: If we are successful, we will finish the summer feeling inspired as volunteers and cohesive as a team. We will see measurable positive effects on the majority of participants, and we will have captured metrics and lessons to help guide future activities with 12.14, and beyond.

The execution of the play with an internal leader development strategy was highly successful and was executed **with no plan.**

The team of volunteers was assembled independently, without any common organizational memberships. And the more that the action needs to rise in scale, the more that delegation is critical. Mark Thompson has had curated responsibility for delegating as a component of scaling:

> I'm a big believer in delegation. I believe that, fundamentally, as a business leader, you do not scale without delegation. So, that is the job, I'm a (Peter) Drucker kid, right? It's like the job of a leader is to recruit and develop other leaders. ... scale requires it.

An understanding and use of intent statements restores the lost art. Leaders can use the format of the intent statement for more than delegation to subordinates. For example, most leaders work for more senior leaders. They should ask themselves if they fully understand all four elements of *their* leader's intent. Most do know one or two elements, but very often there are portions of the boss's intent that is unclear. Leaders should then note that *they* are not in a position to maximize their initiative and their ability to take independent action. In such circumstances, it is not necessary to ask for a written intent statement. Simply ask a question or two that brings out unclear or uncertain elements of the overall intent.

Use of intent in this way was essential in Tom's reaction to a request to assist in a crisis. In 2017, Houston Texas was hit with Hurricane Harvey, a storm that dumped more than 55 inches of rain on the city in two days and flooded more than 220,000 homes. Rice University closed, with approximately 2,000 students left in the dormitories. The university provost contacted our author, and asked him to create, within 24 hours, a volunteer organization that could involve the 2,000 students and contribute to the recovery from the hurricane. The request was a 30-minute phone call, not particularly well organized. In order to confirm what was intended, within two hours, Tom produced an intent statement and sent it to the provost, asking if it was what she wanted. She "red penned" portions of the statement to increase its accuracy, and that gave the author the ability to share it with his staff to kick off an immediate solution to the crisis. The following statement shows the intent that was confirmed by sending the statement to the leader, namely the Rice University Provost:

> **Provost Intent Statement: Stand up the Rice Harvey Action Team (HAT)**
>
> **Purpose:** To rapidly create and deploy a coordinating academic staff agency that responds to Provost guidance and intent, develops plans and courses of action, and then executes to optimize solutions for professors whose courses are delayed and opportunities for student learning through volunteer activities and service-learning processes.
>
> **Method/Directed Tasks**
>
> - Staff with at least the following constituencies represented:
>   - Center for Civic Leadership
>   - Dean of Students/Student Association
>   - Doerr Institute for New Leaders
>   - RUPD/EMS
>   - Development and Alumni Relations
>   - Rice Institutional Crisis Management
> - Establish a four-workstation physical presence in the Doerr Institute NLT August 29, 2017.
> - Establish an online platform that could support the matching of professor requirements and the input of student ability and availability, and volunteering opportunities NLT August 30, 2017.
> - Analyze the outcome of the Rice Emergency Needs Assessment and communicate appropriately with Departments and professors to determine needs.

- Establish immediate liaison with three key support coordinating agencies
  - American Red Cross
  - Save the Children (incl. DINL board member and CEO Carolyn Miles)
  - United Way
- Be prepared to coordinate transportation, food, communications, and security for student volunteers.
- Be prepared to establish systematic receipt of funds (assist Development and Alumni Relations)
- Be prepared to stand up a Servant Leadership Platform: offer students curricula on civic engagement and serving leadership (assist Center for Civic Leadership and Center for Teaching Excellence)
- Ensure that the Provost and her personal staff (Chief of Staff, EA) are informed daily on the HAT activities, plans, and accomplishments.

End State

Rice has a functional team to coordinate the planning and execution of a range of activities in support of professors to maximize additional student time created by disruptions to the academic schedule caused by Hurricane Harvey. Students engage in a range of activities in support of South Texas communities, in particular the City of Houston. Schools, Departments, professors and the HAT coordinate to maximize learning by students. The Doerr Institute for New Leaders establishes appropriate leader development strategies for interested students. Rice is made better by the opportunity that Hurricane Harvey represents, and provides meaningful support to the short-term needs of the community. By December 2017, the HAT is prepared to transition to a permanent staff agency to maximize volunteerism, service learning, and leader development among students at Rice University.

Within 48 hours, the team of volunteers, numbering more than 1,800 students, was created and began assisting in the recovery from Hurricane Harvey. They took the carpeting and drywall out of more than 80 homes. They put together more than 31,000 meals at the Houston Food Bank. They assisted in the support of more than 15,000 displaced Houstonians in a convention center. The volunteer organization successfully transitioned into a permanent staff agency for future volunteer activities endorsed by the university. All the goals were achieved with no plan—only the intent statement and active initiative in the face of the crisis.

General Hertling is aligned with the notion of empowerment plus specificity in guidance. He makes it clear:

> (Empowerment occurs) with more direct assignment of responsibility. And at least in the healthcare organization I work for, no one was taking notes. No one was being assigned specific responsibility. And very few were told when they needed it, when the boss, the leader, needed it by so in a crisis, I think you delegate more, but with specificity and a required timeline, and that's what makes the difference, because as a leader, you're trying to synchronize those actions to overcome the challenge, and you can't afford to wait for someone to be on their own timeline. You have to make sure that they understand what the matrix of decision making is and how you synchronize action so before you make a decision, why you have to have action M completed on the other end of the spectrum.

How to Formulate and Deliver Your First Intent Statement

One important aspect of leadership that makes it easier to lead by intent is termed "presumption of competence." Presuming competence is the belief that all individuals, regardless of their background or perceived abilities, are capable of learning, understanding, and thinking. It means interacting with others as you would with anyone else, treating them with respect and as equals, and providing them with age-appropriate materials and opportunities. It's the idea that even if someone communicates differently or doesn't outwardly show comprehension, they still possess the capacity to learn and understand. Presumption of competence places the leader in the direction of solutions by follower empowerment. Leaders who presume competence connect well with their people. In a sense, presumption of competence is another phrase for the word "trust."

Here's a more detailed explanation:

- **Core Belief:** Presuming competence is a fundamental belief that everyone has the capacity to learn, grow, and understand.
- **Respectful Interaction:** It involves interacting with individuals in a respectful and age-appropriate manner, just as you would with anyone else.
- **Beyond Communication:** It's not just about what you see or hear; it's about recognizing that a person's ability to communicate doesn't define their capacity to understand.
- **Impact on Learning:** When we presume competence, we create a positive learning environment that encourages exploration, participation, and growth.
- **Eliminating Harm:** Presuming incompetence can be harmful, as it can limit opportunities and hinder a person's potential.
- **Inclusive Approach:** Presuming competence is a key component of inclusive education and is rooted in human rights principles.

- **Practical Application:** In practice, this means providing access to age-appropriate materials, engaging in open communication, and creating opportunities for participation and interaction.

It should be noted that presumption of competence does not mean no accountability. As is the case in Chapter 12 and the management of failure, accountability is still necessary and important. Yet when done with followers we presume to be competent, the accountability is likely to address issues in the organization that contributed to the problem, less so than focusing on an individual as the problem. By doing that, the solution is likely to help everyone in the organization. In addition, when looking at the individual, accountability is more likely to be viewed as event based, or even bad luck, rather than viewing the problem as a permanent characteristic of the individual. Unless the organization's HR hiring process is poor, an individual is far more likely to be competent than incompetent and the sole source of a bad outcome. Fix the problem, with attempting to fix the person as a last resort.

The use of intent statements to improve or replace plans is essential for leading in uncertainty and crisis—or more ordinary circumstances. That said, useful and successfully executable plans are equally valuable. In the next chapter, we look directly at how to avoid plans that are flawed or poorly executable.

CHAPTER

9

Avoiding Accepting a Flawed Plan

In this chapter, we will answer the question, "How best can a leader avoid accepting a flawed plan?" The need is particularly true in conditions of uncertainty and crisis, where plans often must be hastily compiled, and when planning decisions are often made with minimal or questionable knowledge.

Have you ever been on a planning team, or watched a plan come together in an organization? Assuming that the team is well led, the outcome is a plan composed with professionalism, confidence, and a degree of pride. The plan represents many hours of work. The plan is based on both research by the team, and the personal experience of its members. They own it. Their professional reputations are enhanced by the quality of the plan that they composed. When briefing the plan to organizational leadership, the planning team is not neutral; they sell it, and they sell themselves.

The pride of planners makes the plan they give to their CEOs or other senior leadership like a baby—and no one can say a baby is ugly. Criticism of a plan by those outside the planning team is very hard to do without creating a large amount of friction. The resistance to criticism is often internal to the team as well. To criticize the plan is seen as criticizing the team itself. Particular team members tend to associate with the design of specific elements of the plan, so to criticize those can be viewed as a direct personal attack.

Leader Management of Groupthink

Plans are all necessarily based on assumptions. Uncertainty is characterized by a lack of confidence in assumptions. Assumptions are still necessary, but uncertainty places their validity in question. Because of the aspect of assumptions, planning has to be very carefully assessed, especially under conditions of uncertainty. Taking in and attempting to execute plans when uncertainty is occurring is highly vulnerable to mistakes. And the group that created the plan thinks it has no mistakes, or they would not have finalized and briefed it. This creates the conditions for a condition referred to as groupthink.

Planning teams are often a perfect storm for the creation of groupthink, a psychological phenomenon that occurs within a group of people when the desire for harmony or conformity in the group results in an irrational or dysfunctional decision-making outcome. Coined by social psychologist Irving Janis in 1972, it describes a situation where group members, often to avoid conflict or express dissenting opinions, suppress their own critical thinking in favor of a perceived consensus. This can lead to flawed decisions, as alternative viewpoints and potential risks are not adequately explored.

Janis identified several key symptoms that indicate groupthink is at play:

- **Illusion of Invulnerability:** Group members develop excessive optimism that encourages taking extreme risks.
- **Collective Rationalization:** Members discount warnings and do not reconsider their assumptions.
- **Belief in Inherent Morality:** Members believe in the rightness of their cause and therefore ignore the ethical or moral consequences of their decisions.
- **Stereotyped Views of Out-groups:** Negative views of "enemy" or opposing groups make effective responses to conflict seem unnecessary.
- **Direct Pressure on Dissenters:** Members are under pressure not to express arguments against any of the group's views.
- **Self-censorship:** Doubts and deviations from the perceived group consensus are not expressed.
- **Illusion of Unanimity:** The majority view and judgments are assumed to be unanimous. Silence is often mistaken for agreement.
- **Self-appointed "Mindguards":** Members protect the group and the leader from information that is problematic or contradictory to the group's cohesiveness, view, and/or decisions.

Several conditions can foster groupthink:

- **High Group Cohesiveness:** While generally positive, strong group unity can lead members to prioritize maintaining that unity over making sound judgments.

- **Directive Leadership:** A leader who clearly states their preferences early on can discourage dissenting opinions.
- **Isolation of the Group:** Lack of exposure to outside opinions or alternative perspectives can reinforce the group's initial biases.
- **Stressful Situations:** When groups are under significant pressure or facing a crisis, the desire for a quick and unified decision can override critical evaluation.
- **Lack of Impartial Leadership:** Leaders who promote a preferred solution can steer the group toward it, regardless of its merits.
- **Homogeneity of Members' Social Background and Ideology:** Similar backgrounds and beliefs can lead to a narrow range of perspectives.

Groupthink can lead to a range of detrimental outcomes in planning:

- **Poor Decision-making:** The failure to consider alternatives and risks often results in suboptimal or even disastrous choices.
- **Inadequate Contingency Planning:** Overconfidence can lead to a lack of preparation for potential negative outcomes.
- **Suppression of Innovation and Creativity:** Individual creativity and critical thinking are stifled in favor of conformity.
- **Ethical Lapses:** The belief in the group's inherent morality can lead to the justification of unethical actions.
- **Failure to Learn from Past Mistakes:** Collective rationalization can prevent the group from acknowledging and addressing previous errors.

Understanding groupthink is crucial for effective teamwork and decision-making in various contexts, from business and politics to everyday group interactions. Recognizing its symptoms and underlying causes allows groups to implement strategies to encourage open communication, critical evaluation, and diverse perspectives, thereby mitigating the risks of falling prey to this potentially harmful phenomenon.

Effective Uses of Red Teams

With such a powerful tendency for team thinking to be weak on self-criticism, how best can leaders prevent the acceptance of a plan with flaws? The most effective means is to create a red team. A red team is a group outside of a planning team whose only job is to criticize the plan and report directly to the leader. Initially, this may sound disruptive, almost like an attack on the planning team. We are going to show you that it's just the opposite.

When you create a red team, the fundamental first principle is to assemble a small team that is fully independent of the influence of the planning staff. Their sole purpose is to criticize the plan as it is developed, and to share their criticisms with the organization's leader, not the planning team. Importantly, the red team does *not* propose solutions to the problems they uncover, that's the responsibility of the planning team, which is in a much better position to do so once the problem is uncovered. Otherwise, the red team becomes a sort of secondary planning team.

The red team is a fresh set of eyes, immune to the inherent politics of criticism and the barriers of groupthink. The leader is then responsible for deciding what to share with the planning team and how to share it. The leader can ease the criticisms into the dialogue, preventing the perception that the red team is attacking the planning team. This allows for simple changes to the plan as it is formed rather than creating the conditions for problems in the plan to be revealed as the final plan is briefed. Often the best way is for the leader to formulate some questions that cause the planning team to relook portions of the plan and come up with their own recognitions of the problems and their own solutions—plan improvement is seen as their work, not an order from the top. Mark Thompson holds considerable respect for the use of red teams:

> Red team, blue teams are really great in terms of being able to set. Adobe does that all the time. Amazon is still doing it, at Schwab, we did it a lot. Well, basically you got, you got the guys who are doing incremental change and the people who are trying to destroy the mothership with a disruptive change. And so you have the, basically you have the blue teams us, and red team is the other guys. Got the enemy attacking. And so, that's one way to do it.

Red teams can be one person, or many more. One of the authors was on a military red team in the Pentagon with 42 other people—lawyers, psychologists, MBAs—whose sole job was to criticize a major plan as it was formed. It is also important to pick the best employees possible to participate as a part of the red team, for at least three reasons. First, assessing the development of a plan is a difficult job, and it takes original, independent, creative thinkers to do it well. Second, the experience is highly developmental; thus, to offer such developmental improvement to rising stars is terrific for the organization. Lastly, it is important that red team members are respected by others in the organization, so that negativity does not emerge about their mere existence in the role. Bernie Banks has experience with red teams and the details of their acceptance into the culture of the organization:

> First thing? Yes, I have used red teams. Second, I think flawed process comes back to do you have well delineated process, and do you actually honor them? Some people or some organizations have well thought out methodology, but they don't actually use that methodology routinely. Then you have others that have well thought out methodology, and it's religion for them. If you are in that type of organization, you don't really have to change what you're doing, because you have a well thought out way in which you go about addressing structured and unstructured challenges. Just honor the process. Don't get distracted by the intense pressure that's backing up, or the anxiety that's associated with the uncertainty, honor the process.

It is up to the leader to set up the red team for success, and to maintain their independence. The red team needs direct access to the leader, ideally immediate access. Their existence should not be secreted in the organization, but what they say to the leader about the plan must be entirely confidential. Their reporting should be professional and formal, structured in writing, informed assessment, not weak perceptions of gossip. The leader's role in managing the red team cannot be passive; it takes occasional action to support them, to avoid conflicts, and to steer the planning leadership into trusting the process.

Case Study of a Red Team There are many examples of deeply flawed plans that have nonetheless been attempted, where a red team would have saved the company from ruin. One of the most notable examples of a deeply flawed business plan that was nonetheless significantly attempted is Juicero. Launched in 2016, the company aimed to revolutionize home juicing with a high-tech, Wi-Fi-connected juicer and proprietary, single-serving packets of pre-chopped fruits and vegetables (Juetten, 2018). Despite raising approximately $120 million in venture capital from prominent investors, the venture spectacularly collapsed in 2017.

The core of Juicero's business plan rested on several pillars:

- **A High-tech, Premium Juicer:** The Juicero Press was an impressively engineered machine, initially priced at $699 (later reduced to $399). It boasted aircraft-grade aluminum and a complex mechanism to exert several tons of force to extract juice from the packets. It was also Wi-Fi connected, a feature ostensibly for quality control and to ensure packets weren't expired, though its necessity was widely questioned.
- **Proprietary, Subscription-based Packets:** Consumers could only use Juicero's own pre-filled packets of organic fruits and vegetables, priced between $5 and $7 each. These were marketed for their convenience and freshness, delivered via a subscription model.
- **A Closed Ecosystem:** The juicer would only work with Juicero's packets, which featured a QR code that the machine scanned. This created a "Keurig-for-juice" model, locking consumers into their ecosystem.

The deep flaws in Juicero's business plan were eventually quite obvious. The most glaring flaw, and the one that ultimately sealed its fate, was the revelation that the Juicero packets could be squeezed by hand to yield nearly the same amount of juice, in a comparable amount of time, as the expensive machine. This immediately rendered the core value proposition of the high-tech, costly juicer almost entirely moot. Why invest in a $400–$700 machine when your hands would suffice? As examined in *Forbes*,

> The biggest issue the Juicero faced was that it didn't improve upon the oldest juicing implement on the market: human hands. The company was caught with egg (or juice) on its face when it was discovered that its pre-packaged juice bags could

be squeezed nearly as quickly and effectively by hand as by the Juicero machine, despite claims from Evans about the four tons of force created by the press. And while the company claimed that the press was cleaner and more convenient, and the bags only available to those who had already purchased a Juicero, the revelation led consumers to ask what the point of a $400 juicer was that doesn't work any better than your own hands.

Despite this and other fundamental flaws, the Juicero business plan was insufficiently critiqued, and thus funded and pursued with vigor:

- **Significant Funding:** The company successfully raised around $120 million from reputable investors, indicating that the initial vision and pitch were compelling enough to secure substantial backing.
- **Product Launch and Marketing:** The Juicero Press and its accompanying packet subscription service were launched to the public with considerable media attention, often highlighting its sleek design and Silicon Valley pedigree.
- **Building a Team and Operations:** Juicero employed a significant workforce to design, manufacture, and market its products, as well as manage the logistics of its packet delivery service.

The attempted execution couldn't overcome the inherent weaknesses of the business model. Once the "hand-squeezing" revelation went viral, the company became a symbol of Silicon Valley excess and solutions in search of a problem. Sales plummeted, ridicule ensued, and within months of the controversy, Juicero announced it was suspending sales of the Press and the packets and offering refunds to customers. The company ceased operations entirely in September 2017, just 16 months after its public launch. There is no way that this disaster could have occurred with a red team operating independently from those promoting the funding and the marketing of the start-up.

It is important to note that planning teams often assemble a small group that is devoted to taking the perspective of competitors or enemies, and working to create conditions for the planning team to recognize and control or defend against competition. While such a group may be useful in some ways, it is not a red team. Groups internal to planning teams suffer most of the same groupthink influence as others. Without the complete independence of the red team, problems are more likely to be suppressed, dismissed, or overlooked because of the nature of the planning team. It is also the experience of the authors that the people assigned to such internal groups are usually not the highest performers of the team.

Alternatives to Red Teams

Red teaming requires humility on the part of leaders; after all, it marks an admission that the leader and their planners could be missing something significant. It also requires open mindedness on the part of leaders because the red team analysis could suggest that a project move in a completely different direction than anticipated. It also required trust between the red team and the leader—both must believe that each other is committed to working in the organization's best interests.

There are, of course, alternatives to the use of red teams. One such alternative is enhanced communication about the plan across the organization. General Mark Hertling sees the enhanced communication as a great way to validate planning:

> The first way, in my view, is communicating more. I think communication of all types, and I'll address that in a second, helps you to help others help you. And what I mean by that is, the more you communicate, the more they have a standard vision of what the outcome should be, and you have to repeat it multiple times, especially in a pressure situation where sometimes people don't get the communication, they don't understand your intent. You have to give it to them. Then have them, you know, in the military, we use the term "read back" for possible correction, which is, you know, you tell them, say, "Okay, what do you think I need from you based on what I just told you?" And then do the constant check-ins with them and communicate it again and again and again. I personally think that the active communication, in the variety of ways you can determine how to use it, is the best way to deal or to work through a crisis. I'm going to give you an example. During the COVID crisis we had, I was asked because I had taught a lot of the doctors leadership in this organization, and they were beginning to not wait for other people to do things, but the doctors were acting on their own in terms of the crisis. They established, on my recommendation, a crisis response team with just doctors. And we would meet every morning during the crisis, talk about what was happening in the supply chain, how the patients were being treated, how doctors were being reassigned to cover bases and one of the things we talked about was, I said, "How are you communicating the requirements?" And they didn't have it was just the meeting, and then people would go back to their organization and do whatever they were asked to do ....

How to Get Started with the Use of Red Teams

Red teaming, especially in the military, is often large scale, as many as 50 staff including HR staff, lawyers, and combat planners. Do not be intimidated by that, it is not necessary to create major events, especially if it is the first red team you've built. To get started, it's important to remember the central elements that define a red team:

1. Choose one or more people to serve on the red team. Make sure that they are high performers. They will learn from this role and emerge better for the organization.
2. Ensure the red team reports directly to you, the top leader. Do not, under any circumstances, move them into the planning team.
3. Talk directly to the planning team about why you are forming the red team, ensure that the red team has full and immediate access to all planning information.
4. Talk directly to the red team about their role, their independence from the planning team, and the importance of remaining confidential, and reporting only to you. Establish a schedule of reporting.
5. Let them work. When the red team comes to you with a fault they see in planning, do not immediately present it to the planning team or presume that it is correct. Instead, softly approach the planning team in a routine way, with a few questions that will lead them to assess the portion of their work that the red team views as faulty. If your questioning is done properly, the planning team is likely to cover down on the problem themselves. Tom has done this repeatedly, and often the planning team is left unaware of the red team's criticism. The goal is for there to be no surprises or error discovery when the planning team briefs you on the final plan. The less drama associated with red team assessment, the better. The red team is your set of eyes and ears, not that of the planning team or anyone else.

6. After the plan is critiqued and validated by both the planning team and the red team, reward them both with recognition (minimally) and bonuses (maximally)! You need to reinforce the conditions where red teams are anticipated, respected, and viewed as an integral part of organizational planning. The long-term benefits will be significant.

The more senior a leader, the more that they should have assistance in the assessment of plans given for their approval. Uncertainty and crisis most definitely enhance the challenge created by that need. Leaving self-criticism to the planning staff is an unnecessary risk. If a leader takes the time and effort to manage a red team, they can expect a far better outcome for the plans they approve.

Yet even flawless plans can fail if they are poorly executed. In the next chapter, we move forward into how to ensure that the successful execution a good plan will occur predictably, and deliberately.

CHAPTER

10

Ensuring the Effective Execution of a Plan

Clearly, uncertainty has an effect on the formulation of a plan. Once formulated, plans require execution. Those aspects of uncertainty that make planning difficult—lack of clear prediction, the instability of assumptions, the inability to properly estimate resources—also challenge the execution of plans. Some leaders step back and permit the execution of plans with little to no preparation or supervision. That is a mistake.

The best plans may nonetheless be poorly executed and fail as a result. Management of execution helps not only good or bad plans to be carried through, but it is the primary means of recognition that plans require changes in order to function properly. Micromanagement is not necessary, but preparation and observation are key and essential.

CEO coach Mark Thompson views plans merely as a preparation for interrupted execution:

> (Charles Schwab) and Larry Stupski were partners in building the business in the early days. I was involved with them in the 80s, before we were acquired by Bank of America, and Schwab became a household name, and his quip always was, "Plans never work, but planning does," and that was a way of attaching the fact that you will have so many interruptions, changes, facts of life, geopolitics and a lot of stuff is going to happen on the way to execution.

At all times, uncertainty or not, crisis or not, the effective execution of plans is key—necessary for progress. Leaders are engaged to assess and approve plans, but leader responsibilities do not end there. There is an important time for preparation prior to the execution of a plan. How the leader helps to manage that time is critical for execution. Preparation—the road to execution of plans—is essential. One of the best management tools for execution preparation is called the 10/20/30 rule.

10/20/30 Rule

The 10/20/30 rule refers to the management of preparation time and changes to plans prior to execution. It stands as a guide to control and discipline a leader's direct involvement in the transition from planning to execution. The sum of 10/20/30 is, of course, 60, representing the breakdown of a single, symbolic hour. As preparation time increases, the segments are more and more important. Here is how the breakdown of the symbolic hour is divided:

10 of 60, or 17%, refers to the leader's time to make changes or revisions to the plan. The assumption is that the leader's input and activity will happen as the first element of the pre-execution preparation. It marks the transition between a formative, changing plan, and a solid plan to be executed.

Some leaders do not realize it, but stopping their input and letting the plan play out is likely to be a far more successful execution than if they continued to add inputs. The lead author was trained by the Army and awarded a master's degree for both planning and execution. In the transition phase, there was a limitation placed on changes coming from leaders and planners. It is called the GICOT (pronounced GUY-cot), which stands for "Good Idea Cut-Off Time." Without a GICOT, the people who are responsible for executing a plan would have to deal with instability and last-minute changes in the plan.

All executors, whether in the military, businesses, or nonprofits, need a GICOT. In some cases, the leadership is cooperative. In other cases, executors need to establish their own GICOT and add last minute changes *after* their initial execution of the plan. The execution of a plan should not be a moving target, even in the most extreme conditions of uncertainty, crisis, or widespread change.

20 of 60, or 33%, refers to the amount of time given to the operators to assess, adjust, or change elements of the plan prior to their execution of it. Very often, the people in the best positions to test and determine the effectiveness of elements of a plan are the operators who must actually execute the plan, not the staff that created it. For leaders, it is essential that this review is listened to and, if at all possible, supported. The operators executing the plan hold a unique perspective and often see improvements that others may not. They need their own time for assessment, adjustment, and change.

30 of 60, or 50% of preparation time, is for *operational rehearsal*. Operational rehearsal means a realistic walk-through of as much of the execution of the plan as possible. Operational rehearsal is an opportunity to check every aspect of a plan for both functionality and efficiency.

In practice, what does that mean? It means coordination with each and every person outside the organization that may be involved with the plan. Operational rehearsal discovers that some of those individuals who were presumed part of the planned execution have retired, changed jobs, or otherwise become unavailable. Operational rehearsal includes a check of all e-mails and calls that would be part of execution. Some of the simplest problems, such as a misplaced or mistakenly recorded phone number, can turn into a significant stall during execution.

Operational rehearsal includes a walk-through testing of all product performance, the limitations and opportunities of delivered services, whether high tech or Amish-level analog. Done well, operational rehearsal tests any planning assumptions. It should be an active test of resource requirements, revealing the requirements at small scale execution and then multiplied to execution levels.

One of the best advantages of operational rehearsals goes beyond simply testing the plan as written. It is also an excellent means of testing branches and sequels. Branches are forks in the road, optional operational directions that may have any of a number of causes. Rehearsed preparation of branches can make unanticipated changes easier and give the executors more confidence and ability to move forward.

Sequels are follow-on activities that carry the mission further. During rehearsals, there is an emphasis that tops both branches and sequels for priority of effort. "Center of gravity" is a term first brought to bear by Carl von Clausewitz, a Prussian military theorist who created an unfinished manuscript titled

"On War," in 1827. It has to do with the notion that there is one key and central aspect of an execution that, if won, will ensure success, and if lost, will ensure failure. A focus on center of gravity is among the most important preparations to ensure successful execution.

Bernie Banks understands the importance of center of gravity in his management of execution:

> Always know where the center of gravity is, because it's always shifting, and so you as a leader, always seek to have an influence on the center of gravity. Know where it's at, know where it's most likely to go, ensure you're providing the guidance that helps people to navigate those transitions. Well, for example, in a unit that I was once in, we had a major accident. We had a number of other operations going off at the same time, but that became the center of gravity for the unit. It'd be very easy to sit there and say, "Okay, well, others can handle that," but at that time, because it became the center of gravity, that's where I needed to be. I've seen where others kind of delegate that. It doesn't turn out so well, because they're kind of marginalizing the impact associated with that one thing.

Case Study: Unrehearsed Disaster at Scale

One example of a large-scale failure that was caused, in part, by last minute changes and a lack of rehearsal was the failure of the initial launch of President Obama's healthcare website, Healthcare.gov, on October 1, 2013. It was a significant and widely publicized managerial and technical disaster. At the time, Kathleen Sebelius was the Secretary of Health and Human Services (HHS), and she bore much of the public and political scrutiny for the botched rollout.

Here's a breakdown of the key failures and her role.

Technical Problems and Lack of Functionality

- **Crashes and Errors:** The website was plagued by severe technical issues from day one. It crashed repeatedly, was extremely slow, and many users encountered errors that prevented them from creating accounts, verifying their identity, or even browsing plans. On the first day, only six people successfully enrolled nationwide. "Day 1" should have occurred months before execution in operational rehearsal, allowing for fixes to pre-date the problems in execution.
- **Unfinished Backend:** Crucially, the backend systems responsible for verifying user information, determining eligibility for subsidies, and transmitting data accurately to insurance companies were largely unfinished or poorly integrated. This led to inaccurate determinations and issues with insurers receiving correct data.
- **Insufficient Operational Rehearsal:** The website was launched without adequate testing for scalability and functionality, despite warnings from within and outside the agency. The system couldn't handle the anticipated volume of users.
- **Complexity:** The project was inherently complex, requiring integration with multiple government databases (for identity verification, income, existing programs like Medicaid) and private health insurance providers. This complexity was underestimated, again, a deficiency that would have been uncovered by an operational rehearsal.

Management and Oversight Deficiencies

- **Lack of Clear Leadership:** Investigations, including one by the HHS Office of Inspector General, pointed to a critical absence of clear leadership and a fractured project management structure across multiple government agencies and contractors. There was no single entity designated as the lead integrator for the entire project.

- **Poor Contractor Performance and Oversight:** While many contractors were involved, there was insufficient oversight of their work. For instance, the Centers for Medicare and Medicaid Services (CMS), the agency primarily responsible for the website's development within HHS, reportedly perceived one major contractor (CGI Federal) as the lead integrator but lacked written documentation of this agreement. CMS also did not fully leverage federal contracting rules, failing to consider previous contractor performance or designate a single point of contact.
- **Rushed Launch:** There was immense pressure to launch the website by the mandated October 1, 2013, deadline, regardless of its readiness. This led to rushed corrections that proved insufficient. It eliminated the possibility of operational rehearsal.
- **Ignoring Warnings:** CMS leadership and staff were reportedly warned repeatedly by internal and external sources that the website was not ready, but these warnings were largely unheeded.

As the head of HHS, Kathleen Sebelius was ultimately accountable for the successful implementation of the Affordable Care Act (ACA), including the rollout of Healthcare.gov.

- **Public Face of the Failure:** She became the public face of the website's initial failure, facing intense criticism from Congress and the media. She was challenged to explain the problems and took responsibility for them.
- **Leadership Responsibility:** While many factors contributed to the failure, including a highly complex project and an environment of political hostility, the investigations

highlighted managerial failures under her department's purview, particularly within CMS.

- **Resignation:** Sebelius eventually resigned as Secretary of HHS in April 2014, with many attributing her departure to the fallout from the Healthcare.gov launch. Sebelius was a professional and highly experienced, successful leader. She was a two-term governor of Kansas and a strategic consultant on global health care—seemingly the perfect person to advance the Affordable Care Act (now helping to insure 44 million people, roughly one in six Americans enrolled in health care). A momentary lack of executive leadership disrupted her career, yet a single leader tool, operational rehearsal, would have saved it. Operational rehearsal remains an exceptionally important lesson for leaders to learn.

Despite the disastrous initial launch, the Obama administration implemented a "tech surge," bringing in new talent and adopting a more agile approach to fix the website. Jeffrey Zients, then former OMB director, was brought in to lead the recovery efforts. Within a couple of months, the site became significantly more functional, and millions of Americans were eventually able to enroll in health insurance plans through it. However, the initial failure significantly impacted public perception of the ACA and was a major political embarrassment for the Obama administration.

How to Get Started with Rehearsals

Starting rehearsals for the execution of plans is a crucial step to ensure the successful execution of any complex undertaking, whether it's a military mission, a large-scale event, or a business project launch. The goal is to identify weaknesses, refine the plan, synchronize efforts, and build confidence among participants.

Here's a breakdown of how to approach starting rehearsals for planning operations:

1. **Define the Purpose and Goals of the Rehearsal.**
   - **What are you trying to achieve?** Is it to confirm understanding, identify friction points, practice critical tasks, or synchronize actions?
   - **What aspects of the plan need the most attention?** Focus on critical events, complex procedures, or areas with high potential for error.
   - **What level of detail is required?** Will it be a high-level overview or a granular walkthrough?
2. **Select the Right Rehearsal Type.**

Different situations call for different rehearsal methods. Common types include the following:

- **Rehearsal of Concept (ROC):** A highly effective method, often used in military and emergency planning, where participants walk through the plan, often using a table-top model or visual aids, to visualize actions and identify coordination issues.
- **Backbrief:** Subordinates brief the leader on how they plan to accomplish their goals, ensuring understanding of the leaders preferences and intent, and identifying potential problems.
- **Support Rehearsal:** Focuses on the synchronization of support functions (logistics, communications, medical, etc.) with the overall operation.

- **Procedural Rehearsal:** Practices specific standardized procedures or immediate actions, often for repetitive or high-risk tasks.
- **Full-dress Rehearsal:** A comprehensive walkthrough involving all participants, equipment, and resources, replicating the actual event as closely as possible. This is the most time-consuming but offers the highest level of realism.
- **Reduced-force Rehearsal:** Similar to a full-dress, but with only key leaders and representatives of organizational functions involved.
- **Network Rehearsal:** Conducted over communication networks, suitable for geographically dispersed teams.

3. **Plan the Rehearsal.**
   - **Who needs to participate?** Identify all key personnel, teams, and external agencies involved in the operation. The more, the better.
   - **When will it happen?** Allocate sufficient time. Rehearsals can be time-consuming, so factor this into your overall planning timeline. The "10/20/30" rule is a good guideline.
   - **Where will it take place?** Choose a location that facilitates the chosen rehearsal type (e.g., a large room for a drill, actual business environment for a full-dress).
   - **What resources are needed?** Consider maps, business models, communication equipment, props, and any other tools that will enhance the rehearsal's realism and effectiveness.
   - **Develop a script or scenario:** Outline the key events, triggers, and expected responses. This provides a structured framework for the rehearsal.

4. **Execute the Rehearsal.**
   - **Brief participants:** Start with an introduction, overview of the plan, and the goals of the rehearsal. Orient them to the rehearsal medium (e.g., terrain model).
   - **Walk through the plan:** Have participants explain their actions, responsibilities, and coordination points in sequence. Encourage active participation and questions. Test all digital communications or actions.
   - **Identify friction points and gaps:** As the rehearsal progresses, actively look for areas of confusion, conflicting actions, or missing information.
   - **Stop and discuss:** When a problem is identified, pause the rehearsal to discuss solutions and make adjustments.
   - **Document findings:** Keep a record of all issues identified, decisions made, and modifications to the plan.
5. **Take Post-rehearsal Actions:**
   - **Conduct an after-action review (AAR):** Immediately after the rehearsal, bring participants together to discuss what went well, what could be improved, and what lessons were learned.
   - **Refine the plan:** Based on the rehearsal findings and AAR, make necessary adjustments to the business plan, orders, and procedures.
   - **Communicate changes:** Ensure all participants are aware of any modifications made to the plan.
   - **Build confidence:** A successful rehearsal builds confidence and mutual understanding among the team, leading to a smoother execution of the actual operation.

By following these steps, you can effectively initiate and conduct rehearsals that significantly improve the likelihood of the successful execution of business plans.

Be Realistic

If there is a single principle to guide the execution of a rehearsal, that principle is realism. The more realistic the rehearsal, the more it will test and reveal the advantages and disadvantages of the plan. This is true whether the rehearsal is a highly comprehensive and complete pre-execution or just a few tests of portions of the plan.

One of the key advantages of a rehearsal is that it discovers problems that are otherwise unanticipated and unlikely to be predicted. When reaching out to key participants, it's sometimes found that they are no longer in the key position, or that the key position no longer exists, or perhaps simply that the phone number has changed. Laws, regulations, and policies can change, available resources can change, leader support for portions of the plan can change—and there is no guarantee that any of those changes will be communicated directly to planners, executors, or leaders. Rehearsals, however, almost always uncover them.

Assume that changes occur without your knowledge—because they often do. Rehearsals protect you from discovering such changes in the midst of execution, increasing efficiency, effectiveness, and consistent coordination. In the next chapter, we address how to add more permanence to such actions by creating a learning organization.

CHAPTER

11

Growing and Maintaining a Learning Organization

This chapter answers the question, "Can I make my organization better itself and grow under time?" The answer is yes, although it takes deliberate action. It does not merely happen.

Leaders who impact organizations for long periods must create the conditions for the organization to flourish, learn, and grow. Uncertainty limits the number of specific plans for accomplishing such growth, such that the organization itself needs to develop a tendency to grow positively.

Alan Murray begets operational growth in learning organizations using peer learning, reading, and a network of people for the leaders to learn from:

> Boy that maintaining a learning organization in the current environment is most important, and it's difficult ... That's the problem that we [Wall Street Leadership Institute] are hoping to help them solve, because we found in conversations with business leaders that peer learning, peer exchange, is one of the most efficient ways to do that. You know, education is lots of great things. Efficient is not one of them. And unless you're in one of these high-pressure jobs, you can't go back to Yale for a 10-week course. You probably can't even take time to do an hour Coursera course, and disturbingly, a large number of CEOs that I talk to don't have time to read books there, so that the CEO of United Airlines told me recently he spends three hours every day reading, ... but that takes a lot of discipline. Need a group of people that you can be constantly bouncing ideas above and they can and they're engaged in similar challenges, maybe from different perspectives, so you constantly learn from them, because everything you learned in your own education pretty quickly becomes irrelevant ....

There are other creative ways to help an organization grow. The ideas put forth by Bernie Banks are among the most creative and useful approaches to learning in business:

> Absolutely, first (one way to grow), creating scenarios that you put people through where there are no discernible right answers. So instead of "Oh yes, everything must lead to this." One, create scenarios where people are going to have to display the ability to think critically, doing that routinely, so that you're expanding their ability to think critically when there are no right answers for a given scenario. Two, have a robust "to learn" list. Most organizations that people have a "to do" list, I think the best have "to learn" list as well. So, you see some organizations where you might have, for certain leaders, a reading list, great, but you don't just give them the reading list. If you have routine conversations about the books that are on the list, lessons learned, and how those might

apply to the organization's activities (that's useful). So routine reading, creating scenarios to run people through, to build capacity, fostering active reflection. So, after action reviews (AARs), I think, are absolutely essential at every level of the organization.

After Action Review: A Simple but Powerful Tool

Banks' mention of the after action review (AAR) process is important—it is among the very best ways to build a learning organization, and it began as a means of recovering and improving the performance of the Army following the end of the Vietnam War. The after action review process was invented and formalized by the US Army in the 1970s. While it's challenging to pinpoint a single individual inventor, the US Army as an institution is widely credited with developing the AAR as a structured method for soldiers and units to learn from their experiences during training exercises and operations. The US Army Research Institute (ARI) played a significant role in supporting the development and implementation of AAR procedures.

The Army's use of the AAR to create a learning organization and to improve performance in training and operations was absolutely essential. Following the Vietnam War, the US military, particularly the Army, was in shambles. The widespread unpopularity of the war depressed recruiting, both in numbers and quality. When traveling in uniforms, veterans were spat at. In universities, Reserve Officer Training Corps (ROTC) students would carry their uniforms to training so as not to be seen crossing campus. Many of the finest noncommissioned officers were either wounded or lost their lives in the war. Training was not assessed or improved in an effective manner. The need for improvement was tremendous, and everyone who served then knew it (including Tom).

The AAR was designed to be a professional, forward-looking discussion of an event, focusing on performance standards, that enables participants to discover for themselves what happened, why it happened, and how to sustain strengths and improve on weaknesses. Its development marked a shift toward a more systematic and candid approach to learning and continuous improvement within the military.

Influences that predate the formalized AAR and set the stage for its development include S. L. A. Marshall's "interviews after combat" conducted during World War II and the "performance critiques" that were used in the military prior to the 1970s. However, the AAR process as it is understood and widely adopted today originated with the US Army's efforts in the 1970s.

Case Study: A Legacy of Principled and Practical Leader Development

Lieutenant General (Retired) Walter F. Ulmer Jr. is a highly respected figure in the field of leader development, renowned for his extensive experience in both the US Army and as president and CEO of the Center for Creative Leadership (CCL). His work emphasizes a principled yet practical approach to leadership, focusing on moral courage, the empowerment of subordinates, the critical role of organizational climate, and the imperative of continuous learning.

Ulmer's distinguished 33-year military career, culminating in the command of III Corps, provided a rich foundation for his insights. He was known for his "no-nonsense general" persona, characterized by a commitment to ethics, personal integrity, and a willingness to speak truth to power, even at personal risk.

This emphasis on moral courage and integrity forms a cornerstone of his leadership philosophy.

Tom was on active duty in one of the commands under Ulmer, and remembers small, practical notebooks laying out key leadership habits, including the "how to" of AARs. The notebooks were small enough to be slid under the head straps inside a helmet or kept in the cargo pockets of uniform pants. He recalled that part of his unit's discipline was to check to see if each and every soldier was carrying leadership notebooks when they were at work. It was a major commitment to using leader techniques to improve and advance the Army.

A key tenet of Ulmer's approach is the concept of "power down," or empowering leaders at all levels. He believed in granting subordinates the freedom and authority to act, fostering creativity and dedication. The term "power down" became the Army's term for delegating and empowering soldiers. This philosophy underscores the importance of trust and respecting the responsibility of subordinate leaders.

Following his military service, Ulmer was CEO of the prestigious CCL for nine years. This role further solidified his influence on leader development beyond the military, bringing his practical experience to a broader audience through CCL's research and educational programs. An award, the "Walter F. Ulmer, Jr. Applied Research Award," was established at CCL to honor his contributions to the field and to encourage further applied research in leadership.

Ulmer is also the author of influential works, notably *A Military Leadership Notebook: Principles into Practice*. This book distills his decades of experience into actionable advice, offering insights applicable to leaders in various organizational contexts, though with a clear relevance to military leadership.

His writings consistently highlight the importance of the following:

- **Defining leadership clearly:** Understanding its core components and responsibilities
- **Developing a personal leadership philosophy:** A guiding framework for action
- **Measuring leader success:** Identifying tangible and intangible indicators
- **Understanding critical leader behaviors:** Recognizing actions that lead to success or failure, including the identification and handling of "toxic" leadership
- **The continuous nature of leader development:** Emphasizing that leadership is learned and refined over time through experience, education, and self-reflection
- **The significance of organizational climate:** Recognizing that a healthy and supportive environment is crucial for leadership effectiveness and the development of future leaders, stressing that leaders are responsible for shaping this climate.

General Ulmer's work has had a profound and lasting impact, particularly on US Army leadership doctrine. He participated in significant studies on military culture and leadership, and his ideas continue to inform how the military approaches the development of its leaders.

In essence, Ulmer's contribution to leader development lies in his unwavering focus on character, his advocacy for empowering and trusting subordinates, his deep understanding of organizational dynamics, and his commitment to lifelong learning for leaders. His legacy encourages leaders to be not only effective but also ethical and dedicated to fostering the growth of those they lead.

How to Implement AARs

The goal is to create a culture of continuous performance improvement and adaptive learning by systematically reviewing team successes and failures (Wharton Executive Education, 2021).

Called "one of the most successful organizational learning methods yet devised," the AAR has helped many companies perform performance assessments. And yet, as Peter Senge notes, efforts to bring the practice into corporate culture most often fail because "again and again, people reduce the living practice of AARs to a sterile technique" (Senge, 1990).

The process itself is an active discussion centered around four key questions:

1. What did we intend to accomplish? (What was our strategy?)
2. What did we do? (How did we execute relative to our strategy?)
3. Why did it happen that way? (Why was there a difference between strategy and execution?)
4. What will we do to adapt our strategy or refine our execution for a better outcome, or how do we repeat our success?

The AAR is not merely an opportunity to focus on team performance but also serves as a catalyst for cultural change. To set the stage for effective AARs, leaders must first create a climate of transparency, selflessness, and candor where team members can challenge current ways of thinking and performing. Everyone—leaders included—must openly share where their own performance may have contributed to a team failure and acknowledge the people and practices that helped create the team's success. Used regularly to assess successful and unsuccessful events, AARs will strengthen teams and improve performance and can become ingrained into the DNA of the organization. When key learnings from AARs are shared, the experiences of one team can benefit the entire organization.

Action Steps

Going through the motions of an AAR is relatively easy—putting AARs into the DNA of your organization is the challenge. The following steps will help to make AARs a "living practice" that can transform team and organizational performance.

1. **Schedule AARs consistently to learn from both successes and failures.** "Post-mortems" have a negative connotation that discourages participation and enthusiasm. AARs should be held during or immediately after successful and nonsuccessful events, using the positive positioning of improving your own performance and not that of someone else. There is no purpose for accountability in AARs.
2. **Gather relevant facts and figures related to the team's performance.** If project deadlines have been missed, product standards are being ignored, or client feedback is disregarded in the team's execution, these facts set the foundation for an AAR that is grounded in relevant data.
3. **Make participation mandatory and involve all team members in the discussion**—even customers, partners, and suppliers can be included. Each participant will likely have a different perspective on the event, and this serves as a key input into the AAR. Everyone's voice is important, so you must be able to receive criticism from a few levels down. Open-ended questions that are related to specific standards or expectations will encourage involvement.

4. **Have a three-pronged focus: performance of team members, the leader, and the team as a whole.** Keeping the attention on facts and outcomes, what are the strengths and weaknesses of each? This focus keeps the discussion centered on what the team can control (as opposed to what is happening at headquarters or on another team).
5. **Follow the "rules of engagement."** To encourage honest participation and mutual trust, AARs must be confidential (joint learning is shared, but individual comments are not), transparent, focused on individual and team improvement and development, and in preparation for "next time."
6. **Share learning across the organization.** Many organizations, including Huber and Microsoft, use databases or blogs to make the lessons of AARs available via intranet to all teams. It's inefficient to withhold key learnings from other teams and allow them to make the same mistakes or prevent them from replicating best practices.

How Organizations Use It

The J.M. Huber Corporation uses AARs after every planned project and significant unplanned event. Their AAR discussion centers on what happened, why, and what should be done about it. Following the meeting, employees post their learnings to a database, and an online after action report is created, which includes action plans and lessons learned. Other employees around the world can search the database to find AARs on topics related to their work. Employees are motivated to participate with incentives such as the Chairman's Award for After Action Review (AAR) Excellence, which is given annually to a cross-functional team.

The strategy-consulting firm Jump Associates holds AAR-like debriefings after every client meeting. Employees, including top executives, give each other feedback, offering at least one positive example and one concrete suggestion about how to improve. On a smaller scale, CEO and founder Dev Patnaik debriefed after every meeting and every client interaction for six months. The debriefings gave Patnaik the feedback senior executives rarely get.

Although called "post-mortems," Microsoft's performance assessments have much in common with AARs. They are held at the end of every project, whether successful or not. General participation is garnered through discussions and ensuing reports, which are circulated to all participants through the intranet. Everyone is encouraged to comment. The reports are then open to all so that continuous learning and best practices are available to everyone in the organization.

Lieutenant General Hertling experienced the necessary formulation of AARs with one of his major clients. It seemed to be a challenge initially, but paid off over time:

> AAR, yeah, yeah, most certainly. I presented the concept of an AAR to the hospital CEO, and he said, "Could you run one?" And I said, "Well, I've never run one in this kind of organization, but I think I can get people in a room to determine what are the key things that went wrong, and how did we fix them, or how did we not fix them, but continue on." I said, *"Okay, tell me the things that went really well that you didn't expect when we went into a crisis, and let's not only try and sustain them, but let's try and polish them and make them a part of our hospital policy"* [emphasis added].

Thus, AARs became the preparation strategy for hospitals to become learning organizations, able to face new and challenging threats. Other businesses have been advantaged by it as well.

Tom Kolditz introduced his former client, Goldman Sachs, to the AAR process, and they engaged it aggressively. Their internal leader development system, the Pine Street Leader Development Group, reported significant positive outcomes from the AAR, with the concept introduction/reinforcement done in July 2010:

There were two types of after event reviews initiated by Pine Street:

1. AAR multidimensional surveys
2. Survey, plus track and survey clients six months after the program, one year after the program, two years after the program

These event reviews, used internally by Pine Street, tracked Goldman Sachs employees for progression/retention in the firm. Yet as implemented, they were forward looking, rather than an attempt at backward accountability. They were culture-reinforcing in a Goldman Sachs way:

> Twenty-three firm-wide committees from new products committees to conflicts and business selection committees—most of them look at post-deal analysis—what we did and what could do more of/less next time.
>
> The Business Standards Commission in 2011, while a one-time re-examination of how we do business across all parts of them firm, gave birth to a Client & Business Standards committee that regularly does AARs.
>
> More futuristically, … market structure group thinking about possible scenarios … 60 high potential MDs scenario development on what our biggest issue will be in 2016 (pre-mortems).

Uncertainty drives the need for organizations—including highly successful organizations like Goldman Sachs—to become learners, to become adaptive as the need for outcomes occur without warning. Even the best can do better. It is also important to note that if there is no direct strategy for valuing honest self-criticism, what will occur in the organization is self-doubt, and cover-ups of errors, rather than the advancement of solutions to share across the institution.

AARs are among the most reliable strategies for creating learning organizations. They are among the best ways to turn failures into valuable experiences. In the next chapter, we define and describe the characteristics of failure and reveal the specifics of how to manage failures in a positive way.

CHAPTER 12

Managing Failure in Crisis

In this chapter, we will take a deep dive into the characteristics of failure and cover what leaders need to know about how to manage it. Leaders may view a failure dispositionally, attributed to a person's poor performance. Leaders may also view a failure situationally, attributed to conditions or circumstances.

Decisions about which view to hold are critical when moving forward. Adding to the complexity, it is not just leader interpretations of failures that matter. Failures influence followers, in both positive and negative ways. Because every organization experiences failures, understanding how failures influence followers is key. The elements of failure that leaders must focus on include the creation of guilt, shame, and fear.

What Leaders Need to Know About Guilt, Shame, and Fear of Failure

Interestingly, guilt and shame both have impacts on leadership. It is important to understand the difference between the two. The American Psychological Association (APA) defines guilt as "a self-conscious emotion characterized by a painful appraisal of having done (or thought) something that is wrong and often by a readiness to take action designed to undo or mitigate this wrong." It is distinct from shame, in which there is the additional strong fear of one's deeds being publicly exposed to judgment or ridicule.

Guilt is a gift we give ourselves; our values and self-assessments are what cause us to feel guilty. Being conscientious and responsible can cause us to feel guilty when we perform poorly or have a failure. Research has shown that feeling guilty may actually enhance leadership. Stanford professor Francis Flynn and his coauthor Rebecca Schaumberg say that guilt-prone individuals may make better leaders. In their study, they administered personality tests to groups of four or five people. The tests measured guilt proneness, shame proneness, extraversion, and other traits. The groups were then asked to perform two group tasks, such as developing a marketing campaign for launching a product. For each group, the researchers deliberately avoided designating a leader.

After the tasks were complete, participants rated one another on leadership qualities, such as taking charge of the task or facilitating the discussion. These qualities would have had to arise naturally given the initial leaderless-ness of the groups. Flynn and Schaumberg found that an individual's guilt proneness actually predicted emerging leadership more than even extraversion, a well-known predictor of leadership in tasks such as these (Schaumberg and Flynn, 2012).

We often use the words *shame* and *guilt* interchangeably, but this causes problems. If we avoid tough conversations in order to save someone from *shame*, what we actually might be doing is avoiding important information that simply makes someone feel a little guilt. In a nutshell:

- **Guilt**: "I did something bad."
- **Shame**: "I *am* bad, and people know it."

Guilt is the knowledge that when I've done something bad, I can do better next time. Shame is the understanding that if I *am* bad, there's no hope for me. The best leaders ensure that shame does not exist in their organization, and that when their people feel guilty because of a failure, that it is a motivation to do better, rather than stay the same.

Shame has dangerous effects because it's not about the behavior; it's about the entirety of the person. Avoiding tough conversations because of the fear of shame puts people back into their armor and away from productive conflict. As Brene Brown says, "Shame corrodes the very part of us that believes we are capable of change" (Brown, 2007).

Guilt, on the other hand, is a compass for moral behavior. It's okay to feel this if you've done something wrong. Guilt is about behavior, and behavior can be changed for next time. Changing our behaviors is about personal growth, which is what leaders ultimately want for themselves and others. As described by Brown: "Guilt is just as powerful, but its influence is positive, while shame is destructive" (Brown, 2018).

In fact, the fear of shame can lead people into behaviors resembling narcissism. Brown defines narcissism as "the shame-based fear of being ordinary." But more than that, shame is highly correlated to addictions, depression, bullying, and mental illness. Guilt is inversely correlated to those. Guilt is simply the disconnection between actions and values. And guilt can even provoke empathy, which is the antidote to shame.

So, leaders should use care in the words they use with others. They emphasize behavior, not personal character. They help determine how their followers internalize what was said. Others being held accountable for behavior is different than being shamed into hopelessness.

Conscientiousness, which can feed guilt, is one of the Big Five personality traits associated with high-quality leadership. The Big Five traits are among the most researched personality variables in history, and they include Openness, Conscientiousness, Extraversion, Agreeableness, and Neuroticism—creating the acronym "OCEAN" (McCrae, 1987).

Of all the traits, Conscientiousness is the one that mostly affects leadership in a positive way. In terms of leader development, it's important to note that personality variables tend not to change over time, the nature of personality measures is that they are *enduring*. Coaching and other leader development processes may take personality into account in various ways, but the personality of the person being developed is unlikely to change.

Shame, however, has a much different effect on organizations and leadership. Shame, by definition, is publicly influenced. We do not give ourselves shame in the way we create guilt. Shame is placed upon us by others. Some heavily assessed organizations develop into shame cultures, where people internal to the organization routinely criticize one another as a form of accountability. It is little wonder that trust erodes in such circumstances. Most leaders recognize the importance of having accountability discussions and criticizing performance in private rather than in public. Public criticism is shaming. It is terrible for organizational leadership and creates multiple negative conditions in organizations. Dr. June Price Tangney, a clinical psychologist and professor of psychology at George Mason University, clarifies the primary difference between guilt and shame in an APA interview. Tangney says that guilt is related to a specific behavior, while shame is related to your whole self, implying a sense of being fundamentally flawed.

For example, guilt might lead you to feel bad about saying something unkind to a friend or engaging in another hurtful behavior. It may also drive you to apologize and avoid speaking to them in this way in the future, better aligning your vacations with your values and your moral compass. In this context, you may feel that you're a generally good person who did something bad or regretful. A person who feels ashamed, on the other hand, might cast themselves in a completely negative light, feeling that they're a bad person for making that mistake.

Mark Thompson has a clear understanding of why failure—in particular rapid failure followed by change—is not necessarily a source of guilt and definitely not a source of shame. His experiences have been powerful:

> Instead of identifying the people with the failure, identify the problem with the failure, and then, iterate, kind of iterate forward, alright? So it's basically feedback, not futile, futility or finality, basically, right? That's what failure is supposed to be.

Recall that the after action review (AAR) process described in the last chapter encourages people who make mistakes to admit them during the AAR process—in public. Leaders who accept that and focus on how to improve next time, rather than finger-pointing, and thus develop the exact opposite of a shame culture. People admit their mistakes, and likely feel somewhat guilty, but the rest of the organization respects their honesty and focuses on improvement instead of peer criticism.

Insofar as AARs are a method of improvement, and of creating a learning organization, shaming is just the opposite; it stifles willingness to admit errors and prevents the organization from improving itself. Alan Murray appreciates the value of failure and its creation of hope in this quote:

> Have to view failures as an opportunity, opportunity to learn, to route what the lessons of the failure are, and move on. I'll tell you the other quote in this conversation that I just had with Udo, a line that he said at the London conference. He said, "the leaders just to define reality and divide hope." That's another way I think, of saying the same thing, that after a failure, you need to very quickly understand what's wrong, understand what you can learn from it, but come out of it with a sense of hope for the future.

Sometimes guilt, and always shame, will affect how individuals view failures, thus it is extremely important that leaders understand both feelings and manage how they emerge in teams or the organization. As young people age, their experiences with failure and guilt/shame result in either confidence or in fear of failure. So, what is fear of failure?

Fear of Failure

The best way to understand the nature of fear of failure is to focus on the elements of measuring it, looking directly at how psychologists define and determine how much fear of failure a person has. Fear of failure is treated as a personality trait, thus it has a degree of enduring existence. Measuring fear of failure involves evaluating thoughts, feelings, and behaviors linked to the fear of failure (Conroy, 2002).

Various psychometric tools have been developed to quantify this fear, allowing researchers and clinicians to understand its intensity and dimensions in individuals.

The Performance Failure Appraisal Inventory (PFAI) is one of the most widely used and reliable tools for this purpose. This assessment aids in identifying the most significant elements of fear of failure across various dimensions, leading to more focused and effective treatments. The PFAI is a scientifically backed and reliable test designed to measure fear of failure across multiple dimensions. It has been utilized in various trials and scientific research studies.

The test consists of 25 items, rated on a Likert scale from 1 (Strongly Disagree) to 5 (Strongly Agree), covering 5 key dimensions, in addition to the general fear of failure:

1. Fear of Experiencing Shame and Embarrassment
2. Fear of Devaluing One's Self-estimate
3. Fear of Having an Uncertain Future
4. Fear of Important Others Losing Interest
5. Fear of Upsetting Important Others

If you read through the measurement of fear of failure, it will become more obvious to you how it develops in individuals and how it is likely to influence their performance. All coaches should have a good sense for statements that raise a red flag about their client's concern for failure. Here are the questions that examine fear of failure:

1. When I am failing, it is often because I am not smart enough to perform successfully.
2. When I am failing, my future seems uncertain.
3. When I am failing, it upsets important others.
4. When I am failing, I blame my lack of talent.
5. When I am failing, I believe that my future plans will change.
6. When I am failing, I expect to be criticized by important others.
7. When I am failing, I am afraid that I might not have enough talent.

8. When I am failing, it upsets my "plan" for the future.
9. When I am failing, I lose the trust of people who are important to me.
10. When I am not succeeding, I am less valuable than when I succeed.
11. When I am not succeeding, people are less interested in me.
12. When I am failing, I am not worried about it affecting my future plans.
13. When I am not succeeding, people seem to want to help me less.
14. When I am failing, important others are not happy.
15. When I am not succeeding, I get down on myself easily.
16. When I am failing, I hate the fact that I am not in control of the outcome.
17. When I am not succeeding, people tend to leave me alone.
18. When I am failing, it is embarrassing if others are there to see it.
19. When I am failing, important others are disappointed.
20. When I am failing, I believe that everybody knows I am failing.
21. When I am not succeeding, some people are not interested in me anymore.
22. When I am failing, I believe that my doubters feel that they were right about me.
23. When I am not succeeding, my value decreases for some people.
24. When I am failing, I worry about what others think about me.

25. When I am failing, I worry that others may think I am not trying

Following are the questions, organized and clustered to show the five key dimensions. The purpose of laying these out in clusters reveals details about the nature of each dimension.

Fear of Experiencing Shame and Embarrassment

10. When I am not succeeding, I am less valuable than when I succeed.
15. When I am not succeeding, I get down on myself easily.
18. When I am failing, it is embarrassing if others are there to see it.
20. When I am failing, I believe that everybody knows I am failing.
22. When I am failing, I believe that my doubters feel that they were right about me.
24. When I am failing, I worry about what others think about me.
25. When I am failing, I worry that others may think I am not trying.

Fear of Devaluing One's Self-estimate

1. When I am failing, it is often because I am not smart enough to perform successfully.
4. When I am failing, I blame my lack of talent.
7. When I am failing, I am afraid that I might not have enough talent.
16. When I am failing, I hate the fact that I am not in control of the outcome.

Fear of Having an Uncertain Future

2. When I am failing, my future seems uncertain.
5. When I am failing, I believe that my future plans will change.
8. When I am failing, it upsets my "plan" for the future.
12. When I am failing, I am not worried about it affecting my future plans. (Reverse)

Fear of Important Others Losing Interest

11. When I am not succeeding, people are less interested in me.
13. When I am not succeeding, people seem to want to help me less.
17. When I am not succeeding, people tend to leave me alone.
21. When I am not succeeding, some people are not interested in me anymore.
23. When I am not succeeding, my value decreases for some people.

Fear of Upsetting Important Others

3. When I am failing, it upsets important others.
6. When I am failing, I expect to be criticized by important others.
9. When I am failing, I lose the trust of people who are important to me.
14. When I am failing, important others are not happy.
19. When I am failing, important others are disappointed.

Note. Items 7, 8, 11, 19, and 24 can be used to create a short-form measure.

Bernard Banks has an important view of how to handle failures. His interview included a very original and creative approach—the simple view of setbacks:

> One, I changed the lexicon that people are employing many times the failures you try as you may have a negative connotation, setbacks. A setback doesn't seem permanent, right? And so I try to strike out this notion of failure. I talk about *setbacks* and *challenges*. Challenges always have opportunity. Associates and setbacks say, hey, we might be behind schedule, but we can still get where we need to go. So, the first thing I do is change the language we employ. Second thing is, was the outcome the result of apathy or complexity. It was a result of complexity; you have to underwrite the setback or the challenge. If it was the result of apathy, you have to hold people accountable. But there is a difference with respect to what created the outcome.

Mini Case Studies Reveal How Real Leaders Dealt with Real Failures

As a description of practice that goes well beyond mere quotes, case studies based on actual failures are highly valuable. One of the best ways to understand leader decisions related to failure is to work through examples of failures, make decisions about what you would do when faced with such an event, and then walk through the justifications for the leader decisions that actually occurred. Following are four mini cases on failures that were either in a crisis or created a crisis. They are abbreviated descriptions of actual events, kept short for reasons of efficiency and also to open up a host of possible conclusions. The ground rules for mini cases on failure are simple:

1. Read each case.
2. Don't worry about too little information. Use the information provided.
3. Come to a decision about how you would handle the person who failed.
4. Pencil-check your decision to retain your thinking.

Let's begin,

Mini-case Studies

In the following case studies, we will describe a real failure, evaluate it, then examine and learn from the actual outcomes of leader decisions. Make your own decisions and see the extent to which your thinking matches the leaders who had to manage the failures.

Failure Mini Case 1: When Getting Burned Might Mean Getting Fired

During a production run in an industrial engineering environment with flammables, an employee returned from break with a cigarette. Peer workers told him to get rid of the cigarette, so he tossed it, but it came in contact with flammables that were stored improperly. A fire ensued, and eight workers, including the smoker, were burned (the smoker was burned so badly that he went on disability retirement at age 20). The investigation revealed safety awareness and compliance in the organization but also revealed some practices that had to be fixed in order to prevent follow on incidents. From your perspective, what are the issues involved in holding the supervisor of the production line accountable? Are you tolerant of this leader's failure?

- **Retain** this supervisor
- **Fire** this supervisor
- Retain this person, but **not as a supervisor**
- Other (be prepared to **explain**)

Failure Mini Case 2: Oops, Nukes!

Your lab has specific regulatory and legal requirements surrounding the safeguarding of nuclear material. This protection includes having background investigations on all individuals who work in the nuclear environment. Within two weeks of a technical inspection by the government, it is discovered that two key personnel do not have the necessary clearances or background investigations. This is a major compliance issue and will result in the organization issuing a report to a nuclear regulatory body in Washington, DC. From your perspective, what are the issues involved in holding the supervisor of the lab nuclear program accountable? Are you tolerant of this supervisory failure?

- **Retain** this supervisor
- **Fire** this supervisor
- Retain this person, but **not as a supervisor**
- Other (be prepared to **explain**)

Failure Mini Case 3: Dropping the Ball

You have assigned a challenging major project to a high performing member of your start up—to create a large-scale training simulation. The successful completion of the training simulation will create a game-changing value proposition for your new company—where you have invested your life savings. Despite offering your team members whatever resources necessary for the completion of the project, it is not completed, and the window of opportunity for doing it closes. From your perspective as a leader, what are the issues involving holding this member of your team accountable? Are you tolerant of this failure to achieve your intent?

- **Retain** this team member
- **Fire** this team member
- Retain this person, but **limit their responsibilities**
- Other (be prepared to **explain**)

Failure Mini Case 4: Justice Following Tragedy

Your global business has its own transportation and delivery company. It is a major compliance responsibility to ensure that drivers are properly trained and licensed. An incident occurs involving a driver who was in the process of being trained, but not yet fully licensed. Five people are killed because of his operator error. A determination has been made to fire the chief operating officer of the company, who was directly involved with the supervision of licensing. From your perspective as a leader, what are the issues involved in holding the CEO of the transportation and delivery company accountable as well? Are you tolerant of this supervisory failure?

- **Retain** this CEO
- **Fire** this CEO
- Retain this person, but **not as CEO**
- Other (be prepared to **explain**)

Mini-case Studies: Lessons Learned

The mini cases represent four separate embroglios, different levels of significance, all different sources of failure. They all hold minimal information about the failures, yet most people who seek to decide how to handle them find that they can still make a decision. Such is the characterization of failures in times of uncertainty and crisis.

There is one common characteristic of all four failures—they were made by the same person. These failures emerged in the leadership career of author Tom Kolditz. Each failure represents circumstances that could have been career ending, but none were; he was promoted at least once after each failure. Each failure represents a decision by a leader to retain the person at the center of the issue. In each case, the leader was approached by Tom and asked a simple question, "Why didn't you fire me?" The answers provide deep insights into the way leaders assess failures during uncertainty or crisis. They suggest that there is much more to firing or retention than the seriousness of the failure itself.

Failure Mini Case 1: When Getting Burned Might Mean Getting Fired

This case was subject of a formal investigation to determine not simply why the fire occurred, but how to prevent such an issue in the future. The investigation was performed by an Army major, Philip Reinaas, an artillery officer who enjoyed a rewarding career and retired as a colonel. His most significant finding was that the fault that allowed the fire to occur was not limited to the unit being led; it was common in multiple organizations. Thus, it was clear that the immediate leader was not to blame, but was unlucky that it occurred in his unit rather than another one. Major Reinaas made clear, however, that the fact that the problem was common to other organizations was not sufficient to retain the leader. A large part of his decision had to do with how Tom had reacted when the event occurred. The fire occurred at night, and the people who were burned were flash blinded during the event, wandering nearby without sight. Tom ordered a medical evacuation helicopter, found each of the seven injured persons, and loaded them in the chopper within 15 minutes of the occurrence of the fire. Such an effective, immediate response helped minimize the injuries and likely prevented fatalities among the badly burned. That outcome was also significant to the investigator in not firing the leader. Lastly, the leader was relatively new, only three months on the job, and appeared to have potential in the organization. Tom felt guilty, yet very, very fortunate.

There are three significant lessons learned for leaders that influenced the outcome of this particular crisis:

- The first leadership lesson: *one can never afford to fire a competent performer simply because they were unlucky*. Such a mistake is expensive, harmful to the organization, and causes fear and anxiety to others who are witnessing the outcome.
- Second, how a leader reacts to the problem is revealing; it is as important as their association to the crisis itself. The leadership lesson: *immediate high performance to minimize damage is an important indicator of the quality of a leader worth retaining*. Always engage failures with continued intensity rather than some form of halting or paralysis.
- Last, the newness of the leader and the assessment of his potential in the organization underscored the value of retention. The leadership lesson: *value to the organization is more important than consequences applied to a competent individual.*

It is important to note that all the facts supporting the decision to retain were not focused on the person himself, but on value to the organization. The retention decision was based on organizational impact and relevance of the leader being investigated, not because the investigator was being empathetic, merciful, or kind. In circumstances where a person may deserve to be fired, the leader's focus should be on the organization, not merely the perceived quality of the person themselves. In that respect, Major Reinaas did an excellent job in protecting the organization in the future and retaining a person more valuable if kept than if dismissed.

Failure Mini Case 2: Oops, Nukes!

For those who have had a leadership role around nuclear material, there is nothing more important than maintaining security around the devices or nuclear resources. When it was discovered that two of the members of the team did not have security clearances, the error was so egregious that the initial assumption was that it was a practical joke. Tom's organization was within two weeks of an NWTI—Nuclear Weapons Technical Inspection. The inspection was unbelievably detailed—down to measuring the size of the grains of sand in the sandbags used to secure the devices. The idea that two people on the team could not have clearances seemed impossible. But alas, it was not.

When it was verified that the deficiency was real, the leader's first thought was that there was no way to fix it before the inspection, security clearances ordinarily took six to nine months to complete. Tom called his boss and explained the circumstances. Tom explained to him that it was all his fault and that he would be responsible for the failure of the NWTI. The boss's first question was, "When did you find out about this problem?" Tom's response was, "Three minutes ago." The boss's next response was, "That's the right answer." He then told Tom to continue to work with the two individuals without clearances, and to do everything he could to prepare for the inspection. Tom hung up, devastated, wondering if he would be relieved of his command before or after the inspection.

Tom was stunned when he discovered a week later that security clearances were now granted to the two people who did not have them. He had no idea that such an outcome was possible in such a brief period. His unit passed the inspection with flying colors, and Tom felt mostly relieved.

However, he assumed that he would be accountable for the ridiculous fault. In a discussion with his lieutenant colonel commander, a future three-star general named Keith Dayton, he learned how the determination not to fire him for this mistake was made. First, the speed with which Tom informed him of the issue allowed Dayton time to fix the problem—something that was possible at his level, though Tom had no idea it could be done. This allowed the unit to pass the inspection and reduced the consequences of the mistake significantly.

The leadership lesson: *never hold back on bad news*—bad news is not like wine; it does not get better with age. Think of yourself as a leader—would you want bad news to be withheld? Never. Yet people often wait, trying to fix things, hoping that the problem might go away. Had Tom done that, his career would have likely been over.

The second benefit Tom had was what social psychologists call the generation of counterarguments. When one studies marketing and social influence, they become aware of counterarguments. The generation of counterarguments occurs when people are presented with a suggestion of influence, like a proposal or an advertisement. When receiving influence, our brains immediately generate counterarguments as a form of defense.

For example, if you would view an ad for the purchase of a certain brand of ketchup, the tendency would be to have a counterargument against it, thinking that another brand might be better, or that mustard would be a better condiment anyway.

When Tom told his boss that the problem was all Tom's fault, the only counterarguments the boss could generate would be, "No, it's not only your fault. You have a lieutenant supervising the team; there are multiple inspectors at all levels of our organization." The immediate response would have been to lessen Tom's responsibility. However, if Tom had tried to blame the problem on someone else, the individuals without clearances, or his lieutenant who was supervising them—then what would commander's counterarguments have been? "Well, Captain, what am I paying you for? Aren't you responsible for training and supervising these individuals?"

The leadership lesson: *as a leader, always accept responsibility for what occurs in your organization, and if you error, error on the side of taking responsibility rather than denying it.* Never trigger your boss into counterarguing why you are responsible, by claiming you are not.

The last element that left Tom intact: the principal negative outcome would have been embarrassment and remediation, but no real damage had been done. The consequences of mistakes do matter, and even had the inspection gone the wrong way, there would have been little to no change in the unit's security or their ability to perform their missions.

The leadership lesson: *the effect on the organization of firing their mid-level leader may be far worse than the net effect of the failure.* At the time, as a relatively young leader, Tom could not see the world through the eyes of his boss. The more Tom learned about his leader's thinking, the more respected his leader became.

Failure Mini Case 3: Dropping the Ball

Tom's failure to complete a major training event design project eased into his consciousness over a six-month period. He was simply unable to coordinate the necessary agreements for participation. In some cases, there were regulations against some of the assumptions given the project; other cases were simply unwillingness to participate. Tom saw himself as in deep trouble for the failure, but the person he was working with continued to support him professionally.

When the leader was asked why he didn't fire Tom, three reasons emerged. First, Tom had the reputational "money in the bank." The leader had chosen Tom to attempt the project because he was confident others could not do it. He accepted Tom's failure because he attributed it to the difficulty of the project, not Tom's unwillingness or inability to work toward it. As a leader, he often established what we now refer to as "stretch goals," opportunities with only a 60–70% chance of success.

The leadership lesson: *the more you challenge your people, the less should be your expectation of success in all instances.* If the failure to achieve challenging goals is met with negativity and punishment, you will see a drop in both initiative and empowered decision-making.

The second reason he didn't fire Tom was because Tom was working directly for two leaders, Tom's immediate supervisor and a second leader of equal or greater power than that supervisor. Such a situation is fairly common in today's nonhierarchical jobs and roles. It put each of the leaders Tom worked for into a cautionary stance, with their professional relationship to each other more important than their relationship to Tom.

The leadership lesson: *the consequences related to a failure are not solely impactful to the person who failed.* There are other dimensions of the organization that could be affected by decisions to punish a failure, including subordinates, peers, and other senior leaders.

The last reason that there was less negativity than expected was that there is a greater failure tolerance for opportunity costs than the loss of existing matters. It would have been great to have completed the challenge, but there was no concurrent loss when the challenge was not achieved.

The leadership lesson: *take greater risks to achieve opportunities, more so than risks associated with routine performance*.

Tom learned a great deal working for the leader who aggressively challenged and supported him continuously. A lieutenant colonel at that time, Tom's leader, David Petraeus, would eventually become one of the most respected combat leaders in the Army, a four-star general, and for a time, the director of the Central Intelligence Agency. He continues to have the respect and admiration of millions of Americans, as well as Tom.

Failure Mini Case 4: Justice Following Tragedy

The tragedy described in mini case 4 involved an armored vehicle from Tom's unit crossing a bridge near the border between South Korea and North Korea. Driving across the bridge in the dark, the 30-ton vehicle was suddenly blocked by a steel girder designed to slow crossings. The driver made a sharp turn in the wrong direction, crashed through the concrete bridge abutment, and tumbled end over end, falling 60 feet down into 20 feet of water. The driver and the lieutenant at the top of the vehicle were ejected into the water and survived. Five other soldiers were inside the vehicle, all drowned. The driver, though trained, was not fully licensed for that particular vehicle.

Tom was about 75 miles away in Seoul when his operations officer called him. As with most accidents, there was uncertainty. The first call said that one person had been killed—and as often the case, the first report was wrong. The next call, two people. By the end, five people.

After the first call, Tom arranged a helicopter to take him to the accident site. When he arrived, he walked the length of the bridge and was met by the Second Infantry Division Commander, a two-star general named Bob Dees. Tom had known Dees for several years and had a massive amount of respect for him. Tom walked up to him, and after a brief moment of silence, told him, "Sir, I just don't know where to start."

General Dees immediately focused Tom onto leading the other men in his unit. Dees said to focus on assembling the organization in four hours and telling them the awful news that five of their buddies had been killed. The notification needed to be done correctly; Tom's unit had the active mission of being prepared for a North Korean attack. His base was close enough to the DMZ that his artillery could hit North Korea without leaving the parking lot where the self-propelled cannons were parked. The organization's mission could not be interrupted.

Lesson: *Leaders should focus on the way forward during the recovery of a crisis, not focus backward.* Investigations are separate from leader influence in the organization. It's easy to find oneself stopping to lead in the midst of uncertainty and crisis. That is a big mistake, and the greater the leader's responsibility, the bigger the mistake.

The next comment General Dees made was in response to Tom's continued emotional acceptance of responsibilities and apologies. He listened for just a few seconds and then cut Tom off. His directive was clear: "Tom, get over yourself." He was steering toward an understanding of the imperfect nature of leader responsibilities. "Do you think that your unit, spread over 30 miles on a hostile border, with more than 150 vehicles, mostly tracked and armored, will somehow be prevented from having accidents? Get over yourself. In our profession, over time, fatalities are an almost certain outcome. As a leader, you are not immune."

He went on to say that he, and most of the senior leaders he knew, had to deal with fatalities that occurred during training and normal operations, in addition to fatalities in combat. Tom had been leading in the Army for 18 years, and at one level knew this. But emotions change perceptions, and five dead soldiers threw gasoline on his emotions. General Dees' mentorship helped keep Tom emotionally stable, focused on reality—a critical leader role to help a follower. General Hertling similarly underscores the principal that it's not what happens that determines the outcome of failure. Like General Dees, he sees the focus on what is done following the failure:

> You know, if you have significant failure in an organization, *it's not the fact that you failed, it's what you do about it* [emphasis added]. You know it also, you know the other expression I wanted to share with you that Marty Dempsey [Dempsey was the 18th chairman of the Joint Chiefs of Staff] always taught me as my boss on several occasions, is "never let a good crisis go to waste," and that that becomes sort of a watch word that I use with the MBA students, because I said, "You know, if you're looking to avoid crisis, number one, you never will." Secondly is what you do with it when you get it. And sometimes it turns out well, and you can pound your chest and say, I beat it and I overcame it, but sometimes it'll knock you to the ground, and that's the failure part. So, it's what you do when you fail.

A few hours later, Colonel Kolditz was standing in front of more than 600 of his soldiers. Both American and multiple unit flags were flapping in the wind. Aside from the flags, there was total silence, you could have heard a pin drop. Most of them had already heard a rumor that someone had been killed. Tom put them at parade rest, and told them about the incident, who had survived, and who had died. Some soldiers were holding back tears at the deaths of their close friends. Other soldiers were visibly angry. But most of the soldiers held unemotional blank stares indicative of concentration and thinking about what they had just heard. At that point Tom recognized how important every single word that he said to them was. General Dees was right. The real challenge, the most important responsibility, was informing them, allowing for grief, and then immediately restarting the focus on their mission.

For months, Tom thought that it was likely that he would be relieved of his battalion command. The incident had been highlighted on CNN. But in the end, he not only remained in command, but was rated highly and subsequently promoted. Later, he spoke with General Dees about the rationale for keeping him in place and not firing him. Dees said that accountability was fixed at multiple levels—the person in charge of licensing was reprimanded. In addition, the lieutenant who was leading the vehicle was injured when he was ejected and was mentally harmed as well—totally distraught.

Both General Dees and his legal advisors felt that accountability for the event was achieved. Investigators saw the licensing issue as rather minor and assessed that even an experienced, licensed driver would have been likely to have made the same error.

Lastly, and most importantly, it was critical to keep the organizational leadership intact as much as possible to restore and retain the efficacy of the unit. Tom was popular with the soldiers, and no one that he was aware of blamed him for the incident. To remove Tom as the top leader would have damaged the organization and, in General Dees' view, risked far more disruption than retaining him. While Tom would have liked it if General Dees was professionally supportive of him as an individual, it was clear that Dees' decision was not about Tom; it was about the unit Tom was commanding.

The ability for leaders to make the most of failures for their organizations is of high value. Failures are like other forms of crisis—seldom expected, but always in the future, a common experience that is most often unpredictable but an experience that every leader will eventually have to get through. Uncertainty is often the background of failures—or they would likely be avoided.

In the next chapter, we move from the challenges of organizational leadership to something far more personal—dealing with medical uncertainty and the uncertain outcomes of serious injury or illness. Like the commonality of failures in business, the high probability that we will all deal with serious medical issues makes preparation for leading through them essential to our best lives.

CHAPTER 13

Leading Through Medical Uncertainty

In this chapter, we delve into the nature and conduct of dealing with both medical uncertainty and the leadership of family in the experience. We will first discuss diagnostics and how medical predictions do and don't evolve. We then show the principles involved in one of the most uncertain medical circumstances: receipt of an organ transplant.

The leadership principles, some good, some not so good, are then covered in an actual transplant experience in one of the author's families. Most people's preparation for difficult medical concerns is with insurance coverage and religious beliefs. This chapter is not about those things and should dramatically add to the readers' knowledge of where they are headed.

The term "where they are headed" is used because everyone will deal with serious medical uncertainty in their lifetime.

There are no exact, regularly updated global figures for the number of people suffering from a terminal illness, but according to the Center for Advanced Palliative Care, an estimated 56.8 million people worldwide need palliative care annually, and this number is projected to grow significantly. In the United States, roughly 90 million people have a serious illness, with this figure expected to more than double in the coming years due to the aging population (Thurgood, 2023).

Medical diagnoses are rarely 100% certain and are instead based on a process of balancing probabilities and managing uncertainty. The certainty of a diagnosis depends on a variety of factors, including the nature of the condition, the available diagnostic tools, and the clinician's expertise.

The Diagnostic Process and Uncertainty

Diagnosis removes a portion of the medical uncertainty we face in life. The process of reaching a diagnosis is a cognitive one that involves several steps:

1. **Initial Assessment:** A doctor begins by gathering information through a patient's medical history, a physical examination, and a review of their symptoms.
2. **Differential Diagnosis:** The clinician uses this information to create a "differential diagnosis," which is a list of possible conditions that could explain the patient's symptoms. This list is a hypothesis and not a final conclusion.
3. **Testing and Refinement:** To narrow down the possibilities, the doctor orders additional diagnostic tests, such as lab work, imaging scans (like X-rays or MRIs), or biopsies. The results of these tests help to rule out some conditions and increase the probability of others.

4. **Final Diagnosis:** Based on the synthesis of all the data, the clinician arrives at what they believe is the most accurate diagnosis. This is often expressed in terms of probability, even if not explicitly stated with numbers.

This process is inherently uncertain because many signs and symptoms are nonspecific. For example, a headache could be a symptom of a common cold, a migraine, or a more serious condition like a brain tumor.

Factors That Influence Diagnostic Certainty

Several factors can increase or decrease the certainty of a diagnosis:

- **Nature of the Disease**
  - **Rare diseases:** These are often difficult to diagnose because many medical professionals are not familiar with them. Patients with rare diseases may receive multiple incorrect diagnoses before the correct one is found.
  - **Conditions with overlapping symptoms:** Many diseases share similar symptoms, making it challenging to differentiate between them without definitive tests.
  - **Diseases with vague symptoms:** Some conditions have signs that are not immediately noticeable or are difficult to describe, which can delay or complicate a diagnosis.
- **Human and Systemic Factors**
  - **Cognitive biases:** Doctors, like all humans, are susceptible to biases. For example, "anchoring bias" can cause a doctor to fixate on an initial diagnosis and ignore contradictory evidence. "Base-rate neglect" can lead a clinician to ignore the prevalence of a disease and instead focus on a less likely one.

- **Communication:** A patient's ability to accurately recall and describe their symptoms is crucial. Conversely, a rushed consultation or poor communication from the doctor can lead to incomplete information and diagnostic errors.
- **Experience and expertise:** More experienced physicians may be better at recognizing patterns and considering a wider range of possibilities.
- **Systemic issues:** Factors like time constraints, heavy workloads, and fragmented patient records can contribute to diagnostic errors.

- **Diagnostic Tools and Technology**
  - **Availability of tests:** Some conditions can only be definitively diagnosed with specific, and sometimes invasive, tests like a biopsy. When such tests are not feasible or available, the diagnosis remains less certain.
  - **Test accuracy:** No test is perfect. Tests can produce false-positive or false-negative results, which can mislead the diagnostic process. Understanding the sensitivity and specificity of a test is critical for interpreting its results.
  - **Technology and AI:** While new technologies like AI are showing promise in assisting with diagnoses, they also have their own limitations, such as potential biases in their training data.

Ultimately, medical diagnosis is a blend of scientific knowledge, clinical experience, and the careful management of uncertainty. It is a process of continually revising probabilities based on new information, with the goal of providing the most accurate explanation and treatment for a patient's condition.

The United States now has multiple diagnoses that are affected or controlled by political opinions rather than dominant science. "Political medicine" is a dramatic and virulent form of uncertainty, and for physicians and their patients, a crisis. Abortion, IVF, treatment for gender identity dysfunction, vaccination for COVID-19, flu, polio, measles, mumps, and rubella—all have political influence rather than accurate medical determination.

Thus, uncertainty in many diagnoses is not limited to the characteristics of medicine itself. A 2024 poll by Sermo, involving more than 1,200 physicians, found that 64% of doctors reported experiencing changes in their medical practices due to politics. This creates a "politically polarized" healthcare environment, affecting reproductive care, vaccinations, and pandemic management, often overriding evidence-based medicine.

Case Study

Diagnosis removes one level of uncertainty, but it raises another. It confirms the nature of the medical concern, but not necessarily how it will play out. It is easy to predict the outcome of a common cold in an otherwise healthy person. Life threatening illnesses have far less certainty. Cancers are, in some cases, likely curable; in other cases, almost certainly terminal, but in all instances, loaded with uncertainty. Similarly, heart diseases have predictability, but seldom certainty.

One of the most uncertain circumstances in medicine is the need for an organ transplant. People with failing organs, whether kidneys, liver, or heart, are uncertain about the length of time their organ will function. At the same time, they are uncertain if the availability of a donated organ will occur in time to save their lives.

The Case of a Family's Medical Uncertainty

In late January 2008, Tom was eating lunch with his 23-year-old daughter, Jenna, in a restaurant, listening to her in a conversation, when she stopped talking, put her hand on her chest, and looked anxious. "My heart is feeling funny; it's running fast and seems to be bumpy." They were both concerned.

After about 30 seconds, her heart seemed to return to normal. It was agreed that as soon as possible, she would see her physician. When she saw her doctor, he did not assess that anything was wrong with her that required treatment. Out of caution, he recommended that she see a cardiologist. Although Tom didn't know it, when she went to her cardiology appointment, which included an active treadmill stress test, less than 10 seconds after the test began, the cardiologist told her, "Stop, get off right now."

Jenna reveals her experience of being diagnosed with heart failure:

> I was 23 when I was diagnosed and told that I was at risk for sudden cardiac death. I wouldn't have a heart attack; my heart would just stop. The doctors at that point gave me medication and sent me home, and scheduled future testing to determine the cause of my heart failure. I felt uncertain as to why they would just give me medication if my heart could stop at any moment. It didn't seem sufficient to ensure my safety. I remember not wanting to be alone. I had roommates, which made me feel safer and parents who were willing to come see me any time I asked. I think a lot of my uncertainty was quelled when my implanted cardiac defibrillator (ICD) was put in, and I knew I wouldn't drop dead.

On March 5, 2008, Tom returned to his guest room at Babson College, having spoken at the President's Leadership Seminar, a group of students from Babson, Wellesley, and Olin Colleges. Tom noticed an email from his daughter—a rare occurrence—that was addressed to the entire family. What it said elevated his concern. She said that she had been tested carefully by her cardiologist. She was in heart failure. Her diagnosis was "idiopathic dilated cardiomyopathy." Her note was positive, explaining that she would need to continue to be tested, had some medicine, but that she could still exercise. For many in Tom's family, that was the end of it. She had a heart issue that was being taken care of.

Unlike most of his family, Tom immediately went to work studying her diagnosis. He was shocked. There is no cure for cardiomyopathy. As long as a person has cardiomyopathy, they are at the risk of sudden cardiac death. For older people, there is a chance of managing such heart failure with medicine, and lifestyle adjustments can stay with them until death, perhaps by other causes. For a 23-year-old, it was likely to either require a heart transplant or be fatal. Tom continued to research the condition, reading medical journal articles, and his assessment was grew worse. In 48 hours, Tom was on his knees, praying to God for him to give him cancer in exchange for saving his daughter.

The family seemed to cope using denial. Several said, "No worries, she has a great doctor." "Well, she'll be just fine." "She's young, she'll get better." None of that was true—though for several years, she was functional. In seven years, she was placed on a heart transplant list. As that inevitable decision approached, Tom learned as much as he could about transplants so that he could lead the family through the ordeal.

What You Should Know About Transplants While Leading Through Them

According to the Organ Procurement and Transplantation Network (OPTN), there are more than 100,000 people in the United States currently on the national transplant waiting list. This number changes constantly as new patients are added, and others receive transplants or are removed from the list.

The vast majority of those on the waiting list need a kidney. Here is a breakdown of the number of people waiting for specific organs, as of recent data:

- **All organs:** Over 106,000
- **Kidney:** Over 92,000
- **Liver:** Nearly 9,000
- **Heart:** Nearly 4,000
- **Lung:** Nearly 1,000

The need for organs significantly outpaces the supply of donors, and sadly, many people die while waiting for a life-saving transplant. This highlights the ongoing and urgent need for more people to register as organ, eye, and tissue donors.

In the United States, the process for a patient to receive an organ for transplant is highly complex and is managed by a national system designed to ensure fairness and maximize the success of transplants. The system is run by organizations like the Organ Procurement and Transplantation Network (OPTN) and the United Network for Organ Sharing (UNOS) in the United States.

Here's a breakdown of the key factors and steps involved:

1. **Getting on the Waiting List**
   The first step is for a patient to be evaluated and approved to be added to the national waiting list. This evaluation is done by a transplant hospital's team and considers several factors:
   - **Overall health:** The patient must be healthy enough to undergo major surgery and the lifelong regimen of medications that follows.
   - **Medical conditions:** Certain conditions, such as recent cancer or morbid obesity, might prevent a person from being a good transplant candidate.

- **Commitment:** The team assesses the patient's willingness and ability to follow all medical instructions before and after the transplant.

2. **The Deceased Donor Matching System**

Once a patient is on the waiting list, their information is entered into a national computer network. When a deceased donor organ becomes available, a "match run" is generated, which is a ranked list of potential recipients. The ranking is based on several objective factors. Personal characteristics like wealth, ethnicity, gender, or celebrity status are not considered.

The following key factors determine a patient's place on the list for a specific organ:

- **Medical urgency:** This is often the most critical factor, especially for organs like the heart, liver, and lungs. Patients in the most urgent need are prioritized.
- **Blood and tissue type:** Compatibility between the donor and recipient's blood type is essential. For some organs, like kidneys and pancreas, immune system compatibility is also a major factor to reduce the risk of rejection.
- **Organ size:** The donor organ must be a suitable size for the recipient's body.
- **Time on the waiting list:** The length of time a patient has been on the list is a factor, especially for organs like the kidney, where a patient's wait time on dialysis can also be considered.
- **Geographic proximity:** Organs have a very limited time window for transplantation, known as "cold ischemia time." To increase the chances of a successful transplant, the system generally gives priority to candidates at hospitals closer to the donor hospital.
- **Pediatric status:** Children are often given priority for donated organs from other children.

3. **The Transplant Offer Process**
When an organ becomes available, the computer system generates a unique match list based on the specific characteristics of that donor and organ. The organ is offered to the top-ranked patient on the list.

The patient's transplant team reviews the donor's medical information and makes the decision to either accept or decline the organ offer on behalf of the patient. This decision is based on several factors, including the donor's medical history, the condition of the organ, and the current health of the potential recipient. If the team declines the offer, the organ is then offered to the next person on the list, and so on.

Living Donation

For some organs, like kidneys and parts of the liver, a living person can donate. In this case, the donor can choose to donate to a specific person, such as a family member or friend. The donor must be in good physical and mental health and undergo a rigorous evaluation to ensure the donation is safe for them.

The probability of receiving a heart for a transplant is difficult to state as a single number because it depends on multiple, highly individualized factors. The number of people on the waiting list far exceeds the number of available donor hearts. However, the probability is not a simple ratio of those waiting to those who receive a transplant. It's determined by a complex, point-based allocation system. It is maximally uncertain; the patients do not know when, how, or if their transplant will occur.

Jenna remembers how she felt dealing with the uncertainty of her future:

The first team I saw, which gave me my initial diagnosis, didn't help with my uncertainty. They saw me as a novelty. One in three women dies of heart disease, and they were looking at me like a unicorn. This team clearly dealt with old men suffering from heart attacks, not 23-year-old women in inexplicable heart failure. When we (moved from New York) to Kansas, I had to find a new doctor on my own. My grandmother, a former Washington University nurse, told me to "find a Wash U doctor," and I did. I shared with him my dream of having a family, and he was confident in his ability to help me. There is now an entire clinic at St. Luke's devoted to pregnant women with heart conditions.

I will never forget the look in Dr. Magalski's eyes when he told me that it was time to move my care from Cardiovascular Consultants to the transplant clinic. They were apologetic and sad, but also confident. He would remain on my team, and that helped manage my uncertainty. Before, during, and after my transplant, the team at St. Luke's has always had an answer. Any question I've had for them, even if I thought it was off the wall and unusual, they've had an answer for and been confident in their plan. When I was officially listed for transplant, the team provided a meeting that I could bring anyone I wanted to. My mom said, leaving that meeting, "Now I know why you're not worried; they exude confidence in what they are doing."

My husband was crucial in managing my uncertainty and still is to this day. He is the epitome of cool, calm, and collected. He's logical, knows how to make me laugh, and assuages my worries in a way that makes me feel like the whole world could come crumbling down and I would be ok. My grandmother also helped manage my uncertainty. As a nurse and cancer survivor, she had faith in the medical system in spades. She helped me to know that if I did what my doctors said, I would be just fine. My parents also helped manage my uncertainty. When I was told that I needed a transplant, my parents assured me that

> we would find the best of the best and go where the care was that I needed. Luckily, I was already there, but knowing that my parents would do anything to get me the care I needed helped me feel safe

Jenna was hanging in there, courageous and confident. Tom was not. Tom did research to learn everything he could about the process and probability of Jenna's transplant. Medical urgency is the most critical factor—priority comes when the patient is on an assist device, close to death. There are also needs for blood and tissue type compatibility, and geographic location also is important, as preservation time of the organ cannot be exceeded. Jenna's petite body size also required a small heart size—a rarity.

The scale of transplants also affects the probability of success—already filled with uncertainty. Approximately 4,500 heart transplants are performed each year. More than *3,500* people are on the heart transplant waiting list at any given time. The average waiting time for a heart transplant can be over a year, but it varies widely based on the individual's medical urgency. Some may receive a heart in a matter of days or weeks, while others may wait for several years, living in uncertainty

For Our European Readers: Ukrainian and European Processes

The processes for organ donation and transplantation in Europe are not uniform across all countries. While there is a general framework and an increasing level of cooperation, national systems and laws can differ significantly, particularly regarding how consent for organ donation is handled.

The most significant variation across European countries is the legal basis for consent. There are two main models:

- **Opt-in (Explicit Consent):** In this system, a person must explicitly agree to be an organ donor. This is often done by signing a donor card or registering in a national registry. If a person has not given this consent, the family's permission is required after their death. Germany is a well-known example of an opt-in system.
- **Opt-out (Presumed Consent):** Under this model, it is assumed that everyone is a potential organ donor unless they have explicitly registered their wish not to be. In some countries, this is a "soft opt-out" where the family may still be consulted and can override the decision. Spain, which has one of the highest donation rates in the world, uses a form of this system.

Similar to the United States, the allocation of organs in Europe is not a simple "first-come, first-served" queue. It is based on a complex algorithm that considers medical and logistical factors to ensure the best possible match and outcome. Key factors include medical urgency, blood and tissue compatibility, geographic proximity, and a pediatric priority—also a condition of priority in the United States.

A crucial aspect of the European system is international cooperation. Organizations like Eurotransplant play a vital role. This nonprofit organization coordinates the allocation of organs in eight member countries (Austria, Belgium, Croatia, Germany, Hungary, Luxembourg, the Netherlands, and Slovenia).

Eurotransplant maintains a central database of all waiting list patients and available donor organs from the participating countries.

This increases the chances of a successful transplant by expanding the donor pool beyond national borders. If no suitable recipient is found in the donor's country, the organ is offered to a patient in another Eurotransplant member state.

The European Union has a legal framework in place to ensure high standards of quality and safety for organs for transplantation. The **European Organs Directive (2010/53/EU)** sets out common standards for all stages of the transplant process, from donation to distribution. The EU also encourages member states to improve their transplant systems and combat organ trafficking.

In summary, while there are common principles of medical urgency, compatibility, and a lack of bias, the European transplant system is characterized by a diversity of legal frameworks, particularly regarding consent, and a strong emphasis on international collaboration through organizations like Eurotransplant.

Organ donation in Ukraine has undergone significant reforms in recent years, aiming to create a modern and transparent system. This system is still developing, especially in light of the ongoing war, but it is based on a legal and medical framework designed to facilitate life-saving transplants.

Ukraine's system is based on a **mandated choice** or **presumed refusal** model. This means that a person must have given explicit, written consent during their lifetime to be an organ donor after death. If they have not, their family's permission is required. This is different from a "presumed consent" or "opt-out" system used in some other European countries, where it's assumed a person is a donor unless they have formally opted out.

Recent legislation has also introduced a nationwide ban on organ donation from military and civilian casualties of the war, as well as from orphaned children, incapacitated individuals, and unidentified persons.

Impact of the War with Russia: The war has created unique challenges. Civilian air travel is impossible, so transportation of organs, which have a very limited preservation time, has become much more difficult. In response, mobile transplant teams have been developed to bring the surgical team and equipment to the donor and recipient, saving crucial time. Despite these difficulties, the number of transplants performed in Ukraine has been increasing in recent years.

Funding and Development

The Ukrainian government has made organ transplantation a priority. Since 2024, the state fully covers the costs of organ transplant procedures for patients. The government is also working on developing infrastructure, training transplant specialists, and harmonizing its laws with those of the European Union.

What Happened, and What Tom Learned About Leading in Medical Uncertainty

Tom's daughter was on the heart transplant list for approximately a year. Toward the end, her heart got weaker and weaker. Her vulnerability to sudden death was high, so she was hospitalized in intensive care. She tried very hard to stay as fit as possible to survive her transplant. She was walking slowly around the hospital floor, more than a mile a day. Eventually, her heart needed help. She was taken to an operating room and fitted with a balloon pump.

An intra-aortic balloon pump (IABP) is a temporary device that helps the heart pump blood more effectively. It is inserted into the aorta, the main artery that carries blood from the heart to the rest of the body. The IABP inflates and deflates in sync with the heartbeat. When the heart pumps, the balloon deflates, which helps the heart pump more blood out. When the heart rests, the balloon inflates, which helps increase blood flow to the heart itself.

The IABP is inserted through a small incision in the groin or arm. The balloon is then positioned in the descending aorta, just below the left renal artery. The IABP improves blood flow to the heart and body, reduces the workload on the heart, and increases cardiac output.

In Jenna's case, the balloon pump helped keep her alive while waiting for a donated heart. It was not, however, flawless. After having it in place for approximately two weeks, the pump failed and had to be replaced. That problem was followed by a second problem, and Tom's experiences during this life-threatening incident changed his ability to handle medical uncertainty for the rest of his life.

The replacement of Jenna's IABP proved to be a challenge for her cardio team. Most balloon pumps are of a size that suits large persons, adults. Jenna was petite, about 110 pounds, and five feet, two inches tall. There were, at the time, no balloon pumps made for small women, so she was fitted internally with a pediatric balloon pump, child-sized. Use of such small pumps are rare in hospitals, and it just so happened that her hospital, St. Luke's in Kansas City, Missouri, had not gotten another pediatric balloon pump after hers was inserted. When the family were told that the hospital could not immediately replace her pump and would have to find one elsewhere, they were frustrated. She needed the pump to stay alive.

After two days, the family was told that the hospital had a pediatric balloon pump on the way from a hospital in Chicago. The family was relieved, and while Jenna was visibly weaker without her pump, she was hanging in there. Soon she was being prepped for the surgery it would take to remove the old pump and insert the new one. She was moved from her bed to a gurney, hugged and kissed by all of her family, and taken to the operating room. Everyone was delighted and excited.

In 15 to 20 minutes, everything changed. She was removed from the operating room and was brought back to her room sobbing. The family asked one of the cardiac nurses what was happening and were told that the doctor would soon be in to tell them. In minutes, he was in the room. As it turns out, when they were beginning the replacement surgery, they had discovered that the pediatric balloon pump that they were preparing to insert was out of date. They would need time to find another, and time was something that Jenna did not have.

Tom was furious. First, there was the mistake by the hospital that sent the device without checking to see if it was on date. Second, the receiving hospital did not check the device when they received it, creating additional delay when the physician discovered the flaw. Tom had a brief, terse discussion with Jenna's cardiologist. It was inconceivable to Tom that such simple blunders could be made in a sophisticated medical environment while treating a person whose life was on the line. His confidence in the transplant team was rapidly eroding. The uncertainty was overwhelming.

The family was told that the hospital was getting another balloon pump, and when Tom asked why they were not getting two so that there would be another back up, he got a blank stare. Tom did not know what to do. He needed expert help. He went into the hallway and called a close friend and mentor, Lieutenant General (retired) Eric Schoomaker, MD, PhD, formerly the Surgeon General of the Army. They had worked together as colonels, creating and writing well-being policy for General Ric Shinseki, the 34th Chief of Staff of the Army.

Eric had connected Tom with a military cardiologist to help him learn about Jenna's condition as it developed. Tom called Eric, explained what had happened, what he saw as mistakes and issues, and asked what should be done. After all, both men were general officers and had spent their lives analyzing and fixing problems and resolving uncertainty. Tom was very surprised by what Eric told him.

Eric's first response was that there were no problems that were Tom's to fix. Eric said that despite the research Tom had done to understand his daughter's condition, that there was nothing that Tom had learned that would place him ahead of the medical team's understanding of what needed to be done, and their ability to move forward. Tom will never forget the principal point Eric made: "You have no job to do except to *love your daughter*. Forget about medical diagnoses and medical decisions. Forget about trying to improve the performance of the transplant team. *Love your daughter*. That's your only job."

Tom thanked Eric and ended the call. Tom really had to focus on what Eric was telling him. Essentially, Eric wanted Tom to simply ignore uncertainty and the mechanics of Jenna's treatment, allowing the transplant team to deal with it completely independent of Tom. Eric also wanted Tom to focus emotionally on his daughter—loving her, exuding optimism, giving her support and confidence. It was faith-based, not necessarily on God (though Tom had prayed throughout the challenge). It was faith in science, faith in medical professionalism, faith that success was more than merely possible, that assuming success was a foot in the door to a positive outcome.

Eric's recommendation was brilliant. Focusing on loving his daughter instead of analyzing her condition and trying to influence medical professionals responsible for her transplant was profoundly better, both for Tom and for his daughter and family. While stress did not disappear, it was importantly and effectively reduced, not just in Tom, but in the family and staff around him. That's leadership. There comes a time in medical uncertainty where research, analysis, and logical predictions have no real purpose. When you find yourself in that situation, lead with love.

The Next Level of Uncertainty: Jenna's Chance at Life

After 33 days in intensive care, on February 16, 2016, two nurses entered Jenna's room and told the family that a donated heart was on its way. It was the most emotional moment the family had ever experienced. They later learned that a young woman in Denver, Colorado, had been having her wisdom teeth removed and didn't wake up from being anesthetized. The blessed donor's heart was removed (along with at least seven other donated organs) and flown in a private plane from Denver to Kansas City. Jenna's husband and Tom were standing in the hospital lobby when they noticed a cardiologist they had met earlier leaving an ambulance, pulling a cooler on wheels. Tom took a nine second video of him. They later learned that the cardiologist was bringing in Jenna's new heart.

The surgery went well, and she recovered quickly, out of the hospital in less than a week. She now has two children with whom she hiked in the foothills of Colorado. Her heart is terrific, but there is still uncertainty. The medicine used to prevent the rejection of her heart significantly reduces her immunity to all diseases, including cancers. Yet the family have all learned to manage medical uncertainty with love. Love is now a more major part of their lives. Jenna has advice for others who begin to experience what she went through:

> My advice would be to surround yourself with people who make you feel safe and are confident in a successful outcome. Don't be afraid to ask for exactly what you need to feel certain that you will get the outcome you desire. *If the team you're working with doesn't make you feel confident, find a new team* [emphasis added].

Jenna asked for another point to be made: She was blessed with a highly engaged family, sufficiently wealthy to pay for whatever needs she had, and she recognizes that not all people have such advantages. She was also given insurance support as the wife of a US Army officer—the Army not only paid for her transplant but paid for her husband's travel and lodging when she was treated.

She recognizes her good fortune and hopes that her advice about finding a new team is not taken as elitist. We know that capitalism-funded medicine in the United States is costly and sometimes simply unaffordable. A 2019 study published in the *American Journal of Public Health* found that two-thirds of all bankruptcies filed between 2013 and 2016 cited medical issues, including illness-related work loss, as a contributing factor. Whatever your situation, understand that people like Jenna are with you, care for you, and have faith in your eventual recovery—both physical and economic.

Such care is not necessarily true in business, or government, or the military, when it relates to dealing with uncertainty, and a leader's performance in a crisis. Sometimes the opposite is true, there are people who may use the crisis as a means for criticism, to lesson confidence in the leader, or to undercut the organization as a whole.

The next chapter addresses the challenges when uncertainty and crisis make leaders vulnerable.

CHAPTER

14

Avoiding Political Takedown

In this chapter, we answer the question, "How can leaders prevent the success of those who use crisis as a means to undercut leadership?"

One characteristic that we have seen among CEOs we have coached is that the disruption of crisis and uncertainty creates conditions for some people to undercut leaders. It's a response to the vacuum of knowledge and capability created by circumstances. It stands, for some, as an opportunity to use the circumstances to criticize the leader, essentially formulating a negative explanation for whatever the leader does. It's much easier to attack in conditions where there is a lack of clarity about why the crisis or the uncertainty has taken shape.

Uncertainty creates a *tabula rasa* that the leader will try to resolve, but competitors or enemies can use to their advantage.

One of our interviewees, Lina Hidalgo, led a blue county in a red state, supported by her voters, but constantly attacked by her state government. Her experience as a leader attacked during uncertainty is quite telling:

> Yeah, what comes to mind is the legislature. So, you know, when I was elected in 2019 we changed the political makeup of the leadership of the largest county in Texas, and so the state leadership, the opposite party, was sort of surprised, right? And so they're trying to figure out how they could stop our agenda because we're such a large population center.
>
> And you know, over the years, they've gotten better at that, but they've tried to attack various aspects of what we do, create obstacles for us to implement programs, cut funding short, etc. Sort of more rhetorical attacks. That'll get us to spend time correcting the record with the media. And at first, my instinct was, okay, well, we need to clear the record on this. We have to not just create it, but try to make it, you know, obviously legally sound, but think ahead of how they might attack it and begin addressing that.
>
> And what I realized is, "you know, if you're playing defense, that's time that you could spend, you know, getting the program done." *The uncertainty allows them to attack and be successful in doing that sometimes* [emphasis added].

As she spoke, she revealed the fact that uncertainty can be used to go after outcomes that would never emerge in a more normal set of conditions. For example:

> This year, there was a proposal to take our water from our main lake, our main source of water, and divert it to West Texas, where they need a lot of water for the oil and gas industry. And, you know, I mean, water is such a precious resource, and it was, it was pretty terrifying and urgent to defend against that. *It certainly would never have occurred to me that they would make that kind of a proposal* [emphasis added].

It is important not to think that attacks during uncertainty are solely for politicians; that's untrue. It also happens in business quite often. We have worked with CEOs who were undercut during uncertainty. In particular, we have coached two start-up founder CEOs who, during a period of uncertainty, were replaced with business CEOs not much associated with the scientific or creative development of the start-up. Mark Thompson describes what he terms, *"the politic of succession."* Here is his comment on uncertainty driven changes in business leadership:

> It's more common than we'd like to admit. And I'd say that it comes up more often than perhaps my experience anecdotally, is exaggerated by the potential Game of Thrones, politics of succession. One of the great complications of succession is what you would hope and dream would be to bring a person up through the ranks who has the experiences, context and cultural connections and a belief in the mission and all the rest. And so, investing in internal people should be a great priority.
>
> So, the campaign now is a campaign that helps increase the confidence of the decision-makers in your capacity to be the new leader without appearing to be increasingly competitive with the others who are being judged for the same. ***And that's where I can see the emergence of some really bad behavior, almost treasonous as you're describing, where you have people, either intentionally or unintentionally, start to play the game of either delighting in the failures of others or pointing them out.*** [emphasis added].

Thus Thompson, the top CEO coach in the world, sees uncertainty as a catalyst to succession. Whether that is positive or negative is based on the particular circumstances internal to the company. Alan Murray, the former CEO of Fortune and the current head of the Wall Street Journal Leadership Institute, sees the undercutting as based on the creation of drops of team cohesion:

> Wow, I wish I had the silver bullet to answer your question of how leaders can maintain team cohesion in the face of uncertainty, I certainly experienced it, and I think it might be the hardest leader (challenge). It's part of why I'm optimistic I won't replace human beings (with AI). That skill is a human skill. There's no algorithm that will ever solve that problem.

Thus, leaders must realize that maintaining cohesion is the best defense of their ability to survive undercutting and continue to lead. Bernie Banks is quite specific about the solution to political undercutting being the use of communications to actively create organizational alignment, resistant to the undercutting:

> I think this is where you have to assign process to communications and foster alignment. Do you conduct a confirmation brief and a back brief, confirmation brief? Did you tell me what you heard? Boom, boom, boom, boom. You send them off, and they go do their thing. By doing that, you can ensure alignment, and you can mitigate the chance that somebody's going to go off and they're going to do things that are not in keeping with your intent or the expectations you have for how they will align their activities in concert with others, but that's assigning process to effective communication in service of ensuring alignment, not hoping for it. Countless leaders don't ensure effective communications. They just communicate, and they believe people will simply pick up on stuff because it's quote, unquote, "commonsense."
>
> Well, commonsense is uncommon. You can't hope that people understand. You have to ensure they understand, and then you have to hold them accountable for doing those things. When people have competing agendas and you start to see markers of that, do you hold them to account for their actions and then say, "Hey, that's not in keeping with my intent, and that's not in keeping with what's necessary for us to create coordinated action"?

Banks is clear—active leadership is necessary in order to stay ahead of those outside your intent. Just ignoring them is not enough. Similarly, Mark Hertling's experiences with political undercutting during uncertain times are exceptional. It includes defense, but as good leadership always does, it puts emphasis on the greater good for the organization:

> I have experienced it multiple times, both in combat and in the private sector. In combat, it was competing personalities attempting to, well, I don't know how I want to say this, but it was attempting to get more resources. And, you know, resource requirements, both people and equipment and units, are always kind of a big deal in combat. And as Marty Dempsey also once said, sometimes you just have to be for what's going to happen. You have to put yourself in a position to (assume) what's going to occur and what's going to be the best for the organization and contribute to it. So, you know, whereas you might be in competition with resources or people or approaches to the marketplace, whenever you have that, you can take a step back and say, "Okay, what's for the greater good?"
>
> In the private sector, I had an experience when I first went to Advent Health as a senior vice president, I had another senior vice president who was trying to undercut a program that I was working on, and I think it was personality driven, as opposed to contributing to the organization. And, you know, in those kinds of situations where it's personality versus organizational effectiveness, that's the time where you just have the candid discussion with the guy, and you have to have the courage and the understanding that you just have to approach someone and say, we've got to work this out, because it's detracting from the organizational objectives. Those are the hardest ones. I think you know, when you really have to throw the flag on somebody else who's trying to undercut you, right?

Handling Political Undercutting

Thus, the use of uncertainty as a chance for politically undercutting leaders is common, experienced by the leaders we have interviewed, whether the leadership context is political, military, or business. There are many solutions—communication is one. The direct focus on the organization rather than the undercutting itself is another. From their experiences, a series of steps come together to think through when you are leading in uncertainty and crisis:

1. Be alert to the potential threat. Stay sensitive to any indication that undercutting may be occurring.
2. If you see or sense undercutting, work to understand the aggressor's intent.
3. Take measures to enhance cohesion in the organization.
4. Upgrade communication so that there is no question in the organization about your intent and the direction you are headed.
5. Do not take the undercutting personally; instead, focus on how the organization could be affected.
6. Once you solidify the organization, take on the undercutting aggressors in private. Focus the conversation on the organization; do not allow interpersonal argument. Seek change.

Understanding the points discussed in this chapter should help to minimize leaders' vulnerability to approaches negative to the organization, as well as to the leaders themselves.

In the next and final chapter, our intent is to track the future so that your approach for leadership is with, or ahead of, the uncertainty that emerges.

CHAPTER 15

What Does the Future Hold?

In this chapter, the future is our focus. Having finished this book, you should know it is not the end of anything; it is just the beginning.

What we have covered has no temporary or limited relevance, it is likely that you can take advantage of it while leading for your entire career, and beyond in support of your family. The goal should be for intelligent, professional leadership to become part of your make up, a permanent and enduring characteristic. It is best not to see leadership as a skill or tool to use only in certain circumstances. Rather, it should be about who you are, not merely what you do.

For more than 30 years, the Army's framework for leadership was called "Be-Know-Do." It meant that there was knowledge required to lead (Know), and there were also skills necessary to lead (Do). It was made clear, however, that the most important element of leadership was an individual's character and values, who a person truly is (the Be component). Always be cautious around people who say that leadership is made up of skills. There is much more to it than that, and this book can support permanent qualities of leadership among all its readers.

Lessons from Katrina

Some contend that uncertainty and crisis are also permanent, that we will forever need to engage in responses to such threats. If you take a breath and assess reality, you will see that in a sense that is mostly untrue. On the one hand, points of uncertainty and moments of crisis will indeed continue to recur; they are indeed a part of our future, that is a fact. They represent an up-down, in-out series of experiences that will continue to challenge leaders the rest of our lives. Yet there is no evidence for continuous uncertainty or constant crises in our lives. As much as uncertainty and crisis recur, they also stand down at times where we see control and predictive ability as dominant. Those are periods where we move forward with confidence, with surety, with the perception that we know where we need to head, and that we will get there.

Yet early on in this book, we revealed that mindfulness and activities that are helpful during uncertainty are also important and workable in times that are routine and normal. As we made clear, a leader can't react to a change in predictability with otherwise never-used approaches. One of the best examples of that is the story of a hospital corporation, excellently led, saving patients in the Tulane Hospital during Hurricane Katrina in Louisiana. Katrina was a devastating hurricane, a tropical cyclone that flooded the city of New Orleans and much of the area surrounding it from August 23 to August 31, 2005. The most frequently cited total death toll is 1,833, with the majority of deaths occurring in Louisiana (1,577) and Mississippi (238). Revised analyses have resulted in a death toll of around 1,400, primarily because more deaths are being attributed to indirect causes, such as cardiovascular issues, after the storm passed.

HCA, then Hospital Corporation of America, now HCA Healthcare, was one of the finest examples of future-oriented preparation for uncertainty and crisis ever shown by a company. HCA had to respond to the devastating flooding that occurred during Hurricane Katrina in New Orleans. They were in charge of the Tulane University Hospital. In 2006, author Tom Kolditz was able to discuss with their CEO, Jack Bovender, how HCA responded to the uncertain crisis. We met at the Center of Ethical Leadership at Duke University, where at the time Bovender was a member of the Board of Visitors.

Bovender explained that an entity the size and complexity of HCA was well prepared in terms of planning for hurricanes; its hospitals had successfully weathered many such storms, sometimes with near catastrophic damage. Its plans and preparations usually led to rapid recovery of routine operations. The problem with Katrina, however, was the extensive flooding, lack of communication, and the extreme destruction of transportation infrastructure. The aftermath of Katrina presented Bovender and the HCA leader teams at Tulane hospital with, in Bovender's words, "a whole new paradigm." The uncertainty and crisis delivered by Hurricane Katrina had been unmatched in the past.

From the leadership perspective, the paradigm shift had to occur throughout HCA in their action to evacuate and save patients. It had to be flexible in order to be effective, and the senior leadership had to make it happen with their own people, with dependency on outsiders only where absolutely necessary. Bovender said two things that reflect the need for flexibility and empowerment in preparing for future uncertainty. One of

Bovender's favorite quotes is from von Moltke, a nineteenth century Prussian military strategist who said, "Strategy changes when the first shot is fired."

Bovender also made a second comment, which fits perfectly with our notion of future orientation for uncertainty and crisis: "You can't change yourself in 30 minutes into something you haven't been for 30 years." The best leaders perform in normal circumstances with precisely the same values, skills, and thoughts that need to be delivered in uncertainty and crisis.

Bovender had created a company in which both leaders and followers held a clear commitment to constant preparation for difficult challenges and life-saving outcomes. They were ready for what occurred during Hurricane Katrina. Such outcomes were well managed, given the terrible conditions in New Orleans, where Tulane Hospital was partially under water. Bovender described the unification of the HCA team during Katrina as a result of four elements that characterized the routine, daily character of HCA values and performance:

1. **Commitment**. The HCA approach during Katrina built on a characteristic value that had been grown in the business over many years. HCA's first commitment was to its patients with that as the hospital's dominant value. The right decisions were made at the personal, team, and organizational levels because at every level, patient welfare came first.
2. **Empowerment**. The HCA response was, in Bovender's words, "incredibly decentralized and empowered, locally." People understood that they could take action because, as he reminded all, it was easier to beg forgiveness than to ask permission. Imagine the courage that it takes a leader to open up that level of empowerment. Importantly, this extended to actions or communications that may have exposed HCA to lawsuits, especially when it came to telling the truth about problems

with the evacuation. Bovender helped set the tone of truthfulness and candor and made it clear he had the back of people who risked policy violations in order to help patients. He made clear to me in describing how he approached policy violations: "I'd rather lose the lawsuit and come out with people respecting me or the institution." HCA was characteristically on the moral high ground because of its clear emphasis on values as the determining factor for key decisions.

3. **Responsibility**. Bovender and the rest of the leadership at HCA did not wait for government assistance from the Federal Emergency Management Agency or depend on it beyond what was absolutely necessary. They did coordinate with state government for the use of some helicopters and for the use of the Alexandria and New Orleans airports. HCA not only marshaled an air fleet of more than 24 helicopters from various sources, but it heavily augmented the airlift with ground convoys of ambulance and busses, including armed security, some of it rather hastily composed. Many convoys had security in possession of guns and ammunition from local gun shops.
4. **Communication**. Bovender and the leader team communicated as best they could throughout the operation using e-mail because e-mail remained one of the most reliable forms of communication. They used the "HCA Everybody list," a corporate-wide contacts array, on a daily basis to keep everyone tied together, communicating and informing. Bovender often answered questions from the company before they were asked, giving his communication an effective and pro-active flavor.

The lesson from HCA during Hurricane Katrina is clear: If your approach to leadership has to change in order for you to be effective during uncertainty or crisis, stop right there, and begin acting with your followers in ways that will carry through the disruptive states with little or no changes. What works as leadership in response to uncertainty and crisis will also work, must also work, in peaceful and predictable times. But the opposite is not true; ways of leading in stable, common conditions will likely not be the most effective way to lead during unstable, uncommon conditions. Attempts to jump into a "crisis leadership style" will be too little, too late.

As we move forward beyond the techniques we discussed in this book, it makes sense to assess the future and to consider how the growth of your leadership capacity might occur. There are reasons to remain confident that, over time, the capacity to lead that you have improved by your current development will increase. For example, when you have improved your leadership in multiple ways, you are unlikely to drop or forget those individual tools, and they will continue to work individually for you, over and over again. However, there is even more value to them in terms of future growth.

The Future of Leader Development Is Bright

Moving to the future, leader development among young people has the potential for having the highest payoff in terms of enduring capacity to lead. This is borne out by science. College age people show higher plasticity of social and emotional intelligence, memory ability, and processing speed than older adults, skills that allow them to learn faster. If learning to speak a foreign language, play a musical instrument, or swing a baseball bat is best learned in early life, then why would learning to lead be postponed for late adulthood?

It is also true that the disruption of the lives of younger people through uncertainty and crisis will lead to their better development as leaders. The Openness facet among the Big Five personality traits statistically correlated the most with higher levels of leadership advancement during the college years, followed by stability or slight *decline* in adulthood. Thus, when we work with CEOs who are in their 60s or beyond, the advantage goes away. For coaches, it is a challenge to fix bad habits that took 40 years to develop. Likewise, the social dominance facet of Extraversion is also greatest among 18–22-year-olds, whereas beyond age 40, no significant increases in this facet of personality appear,

Theory and research on identity formation suggests that the college years might be particularly strategic for leadership interventions because it is during this period when identity is in greatest flux, even more so than during adolescence. We consulted Professor Lara Mayeux, a developmental psychologist who teaches at the University of Oklahoma, for verification of this conclusion. And she said, "The consensus at this point is that college is the best time for some type of intervention because it's the developmental period when most key elements of identity change." What that means is that leader development works better the earlier that it starts in the conduct of a person's life and work.

Time Value of Leader Development

Leader development also has what we refer to as *time value*. The time value of leader development is caused by the integration and assimilation of learning. So, for example, a person who is developed along two leadership competencies, let's say communication and decision-making, will improve those two variables. While each variable has value independently over time, being a better communicator will enhance the dialog around decision-making, and improve decision-making outcomes. That is essentially what statisticians call an interaction effect, when multiple variables interact with each other to create an additional, unique effect. In simple terms, the whole becomes greater than the sum of its parts. Take that principle and multiply it across every competency improved in coaching or other forms of leader development. Growth as a leader over time becomes exponential. Leader development increases in value because of the passage of time. So, when we look into the future, there is time value of work on leadership. And the earlier people start developing, the better leaders they will become throughout the length of their lives.

As we carry forward, we expect to see a reduction and significant change in many traditional leadership roles, especially in middle-management. In the future, leaders must operate within a broader context of geopolitical, economic, and environmental instability and uncertainty. Such uncertainty will demand both flexibility in leadership and the need to be able to balance technology, specifically AI, in both routine and crisis conditions. You, as a leader, are likely to have to effectively supervise a hybrid human-AI workforce, designing workflows that optimize the collaboration between human expertise and automated tools. Leaders may focus less on supervisory and administrative tasks (which AI can handle) and more on high-value, human-centric leadership skills like strategic thinking, emotional intelligence, and complex problem-solving.

You must be agile and adaptable, making strategic decisions quickly in unpredictable, uncertain markets while maintaining transparency with employees regarding financial realities and job security. Effectively leading and engaging distributed teams requires leaders to navigate complexities like maintaining team cohesion and culture across different locations, ensuring equitable experiences for remote and in-office staff, and tracking productivity based on outcomes rather than physical presence.

With high rates of burnout and stress due to rapid change and economic uncertainty, leaders will have to proactively prioritize the mental health and work–life balance.

This is a complicated future, but the knowledge and skills we've arrayed in this book will carry you through. As with all leaders, maintain confidence and commitment to the roles, duties, and values that define who and what you are as a leader. You have already taken the first step in preparation for the future of yourself and your followers.

Appendix A: Interviewee Biographies

The book includes interviews from a number of leaders and leadership experts whose experience, training, and education make them exceptional at understanding leadership in uncertainty and crisis. We interviewed them, and placed appropriate and interesting answers in many of our chapters. Here are the names and biographies of those experts.

Mark Hertling

Lieutenant General (retired) Mark Hertling retired from the Army in December 2012, finishing his 38-year Army career as the Commanding General of US Army, Europe. He also commanded the US 1st Armored Division in Northern Iraq in 2007–2008. Hertling graduated and received his commission in Armor from the US Military Academy at West Point in 1975, and he has masters' degrees from Indiana University's School of Public Health, the School of Advanced Military Studies, and the National Defense University. In 2019, Mark received a doctorate from the Crummer School of Business, Rollins College, defending mix-method research on leadership in the healthcare industry. After retirement from the Army, Mark became a senior vice president at a major healthcare system. He has served on several nonprofit boards, the Modern War Institute at West Point, and as a board member of the Dean's Alliance at Indiana University. He was appointed to the President's Council for Fitness, Sport and Nutrition by President Obama from 2013 to 2017 and the American Battle Monuments Commission by President Biden from 2021 to 2023. From 2014 to 2024, Mark served as a military and national security analyst for CNN/CNN International, and he now serves as Professor Practice in Leadership at the Crummer School of Business, Rollins College. He is married to his best friend, Sue, and they have two sons and five grandsons.

Alan Murray

Alan Murray is the founding president of the WSJ Leadership Institute, which was established to provide peer learning opportunities for corporate executives. He is the former CEO of Fortune Media, where he transformed the 75-year old magazine into a successful multi-platform media company. He also served as chief content officer for Time Inc., president of the Pew Research Center, Washington Bureau Chief at CNBC, and held multiple jobs at the *Wall Street Journal*, including chief economic correspondent, Washington bureau chief, and deputy managing editor.

Murray is a lifelong journalist, having written multiple columns for the *Wall Street Journal* as well as two daily newsletters, and hosted the Leadership Next podcast. He is the author of five books, including most recently: *Tomorrow's Capitalist: My Search for the Soul of Business*.

Murray is the recipient of the Ellis Island Medal of Honor, the Arthur W. Page Center Integrity in Public Communications award, and multiple journalism awards. He was a Morehead Scholar at the University of North Carolina, holds an MSc degree in economics from the London School of Economics, and completed the Senior Executive Program at the Stanford School of Business.

Bernard Banks

Dr. Bernard (Bernie) Banks is a noted expert on the subjects of leadership and organizational change. Currently, he is the director of Rice University's Doerr Institute for New Leaders (and a clinical professor of management within the University's Jesse H. Jones Graduate School of Business). The mission of the Doerr Institute "… is to elevate the leadership capacity of Rice students and to improve the practice of leader development in higher education." Most recently, Bernie served on the faculty and senior leadership team at Northwestern University's Kellogg School of Management from 2016 to 2023 prior to arriving at Rice.

Bernie retired from the US Army in 2016 as a Brigadier General after having successfully led West Point's Department of Behavioral Sciences & Leadership in his final assignment. In addition to having studied leadership extensively, he has led multiple military units ranging in size from 10 to more than 3,000 people. Bernie was selected from over 40,000 officers to receive the Army's top award for early career stage managers (General Douglas MacArthur Leadership Award) in 1995. In 2006, the Apache Helicopter unit he was leading in South Korea was designated as the number one US Army Apache Helicopter unit globally in the Army's annual best aviation unit competition (Lieutenant General Ellis D. Parker Award).

Lina Hidalgo

Lina Maria Hidalgo is an American political leader in the state of Texas. She is the county judge and principal leader of Harris County, the third-most populous county in the United States, and was reelected following her first term. As a leader, her responsibilities are massive. If Harris County were a state, its size would make it the 26th state in the United States, with a GDP the size of New Zealand. She oversees a budget of more than $4 billion. Hidalgo is the first woman and the first Latina to be elected to this office. She attended Stanford University, graduating with a degree in political science in 2013. In 2018 she was elected—remarkably, she was only 27 years old at the time of her election, making her the most powerful leader at her age in American politics. Notwithstanding the label, the position of county judge is a nonjudicial position in Texas. Hidalgo functions as the county's chief executive leader and its emergency manager. In December 2019, Hidalgo was named one of Forbes 30 under 30 in Law and Policy. In 2022, Hidalgo was honored by the Carnegie Corporation of New York's Great Immigrant Award.

Mark C. Thompson

Mark is a four-time CEO who today focuses exclusively on coaching global C-level executives, many of whom are CEOs or potential succession candidates. The American Management Association and Dr. Marshall Goldsmith called him the World's #1 CEO Coach, with more than 70 engagements with boards that are leading vast organizational transformations. He specializes in high-profile roles and leaders, from Sir Richard Branson

@Virgin and Logan Green@Lyft to Evan Sharp @ Pinterest, Steve Jobs, and Tony Robbins.

Mark was CEO of Schwab.com (a division of Charles Schwab), CEO of Esurance (sold to Allstate), chairman and CEO of Rioport (which popularized the MP3 player before Apple iTunes), chairman of Interwoven (sold to Hewlett Packard), and chairman of Integration Semiconductor (sold to SiliconLabs). He was a cofounder of the Stanford University Realtime Venture Design Lab, along with Sir Richard Branson's Entrepreneurship Centres and the JFK Institute for Entrepreneurial Leadership. Previously, he was Charles "Chuck" Schwab's chief of staff, chief communications officer, and executive producer of Schwab.com. As a senior vice president at Schwab, he also created and held the first integrated chief customer experience officer role in a global company, which is now a world standard.

Mark was honored on Forbes "Midas" list of investors as a founding board member of Esurance, Integration, Interwoven, and early investor in Netflix, Facebook, Lyft, and Pinterest. He co-chairs the Institute of Coaching Leadership Forum with Professor Carol Kauffman at Harvard McLean School of Medicine. He holds MA and MBA degrees and was a visiting scholar at Stanford University, World Economic Forum, John F. Kennedy University, and the World Business Forum.

Appendix B: General Interview Questions

To work through many of the key issues for leading in uncertainty and crisis, we asked a series of questions to each interviewee. Their responses were recorded, transferred into text, edited for clarity, and included in relevant chapters. Here are the questions:

1. In brief, how does uncertainty affect leadership? Does it differ from the effects of crisis?
2. What is the impact of uncertainty in meetings, and how have you confronted that challenge?
3. Uncertainty creates the conditions for unanticipated catastrophic events. As you lead, do you do anything in particular to predict or prevent such occurrences?
4. In uncertain times, do you delegate more, or less? When you do delegate, do you do anything specific to empower and foster initiative among those to whom you delegate?
5. How do you avoid accepting a flawed plan during uncertainty and crisis? Have you ever used a Red Team or other group acting as competitors would act?

6. How do you monitor and influence the success of operations in uncertainty and crisis?
7. Have you ever done anything specific to grow or maintain a learning organization, despite crisis and uncertainty?
8. Uncertainty and crisis often lead to failures, large and small. What would be your advice for managing failures in such circumstances?
9. The conditions of uncertainty and crisis can set the conditions for those with competing agendas to try to undercut leaders. Have you ever experienced that, and what would be your advice to either prevent it, or fix it once it occurs?

References

Accenture, & PwC. (2022–2024). Corporate AI adoption programs.

Airbnb. (2020). Company reports, press releases, and news coverage of pandemic response.

Ajax Systems, Naftogaz, Beetroot, Grammarly, Reface, & Ukrposhta. (2022). Internal leadership accounts and publicly available media reporting on crisis management.

Ardern, J. (2020). Public communications and pandemic leadership (COVID-19 live briefings, New Zealand Government).

Bennis, W. (2009). *On becoming a leader* (Revised ed.). Basic Books.

Brown, B. (2007). *I thought it was just me (but it isn't): Making the journey from "what will people think?" to "I am enough."* Avery.

Brown, B. (2018). *Dare to lead: Brave work. Tough conversations. Whole hearts.* Random House.

Butterfield, S., & Sutton, R. I. (2020–2021). Various interviews and articles on Slack leadership during COVID-19. *Harvard Business Review*.

Center for Creative Leadership. (2020). *Leading through uncertainty: Building orientation and connection in teams*. CCL Research Report.

Conroy, D. E., Willow, J. P., & Metzler, J. N. (2002). Multidimensional fear of failure measurement: The performance failure appraisal inventory. *Journal of Applied Sport Psychology*, 14, 76–90.

DTEK, Ukrenergo, & Ukrzaliznytsia. (2022). *Infrastructure and energy leadership during crisis*.

Dungan, R. (2025, April 23). Marriott International's stance on maintaining DEI initiatives. *Forbes*.

Dweck, C. S. (2006). *Mindset: The New Psychology of Success*. Random House.

Edmondson, A. C. (1999). Psychological safety and learning behavior in work teams. *Administrative Science Quarterly*, 44(2), 350–383.

Edmondson, A. C. (2018). *The fearless organization: Creating psychological safety in the workplace for learning, innovation, and growth*. Wiley.

Frankl, V. E. (2006). *Man's search for meaning* (Revised ed.). Beacon Press.

Goleman, D. (1995). *Emotional intelligence: Why it can matter more than IQ*. Bantam Books.

Goleman, D. (1998). *Working with emotional intelligence*. Bantam Books.

Heifetz, R. A., Grashow, A., & Linsky, M. (2009). *The practice of adaptive leadership: Tools and tactics for changing your organization and the world*. Harvard Business Press.

IKEA Group Reports. (2020–2021). *Global supply chain disruption during COVID-19*.

Juetten, M. (2018, November 27). Failed startups: Juicero. *Forbes*.

Kegan, R., & Lahey, L. L. (2009). *Immunity to change: How to overcome it and unlock the potential in yourself and your organization*. Harvard Business Press.

Kernis, M. H., & Goldman, B. M. (2006). A multicomponent conceptualization of authenticity: Theory and research. In M. P. Zanna (Ed.), *Advances in experimental social psychology* (Vol. 38, pp. 283–357). Academic Press.

Klein, G. (2003). *Intuition at work: Why developing your gut instincts will make you better at what you do*. Currency Doubleday.

McCrae, R. R., & Costa, P. T. (1987). Validation of the five-factor model of personality across instruments and observers. *Journal of Personality and Social Psychology*, 52(1), 81–90.

McKinsey & Company. (2020–2021). *COVID-19 leadership studies and organizational behavior reports*.

Microsoft. (2014–2020). *Cultural transformation under Satya Nadella*.

MIT Sloan Management Review. (2022). High learning velocity as a competitive advantage during crises. [Study summary].

Nadella, S. (2017). *Hit refresh: The quest to rediscover microsoft's soul and imagine a better future for everyone*. Harper Business.

Nova Post, & Rozetka. (2022). *Operational continuity under wartime conditions*.

PwC. (2021). Leading through crisis: Balancing operational imperatives with human needs. *PwC Insights*.

Riggio, R. E., & Tan, S. J. (2013). *Leader interpersonal and influence skills: The soft skills of leadership*. Routledge.

Rock, D. (2009). *Your brain at work: Strategies for overcoming distraction, regaining focus, and working smarter all day long*. HarperBusiness.

Schaumberg, R. L., & Flynn, F. J. (2012). Uneasy lies the head that wears the crown: The link between guilt proneness and leadership. *Journal of Personality and Social Psychology*, 103(2), 327–342.

Senge, P. M. (1990). *The fifth discipline: The art and practice of the learning organization*. Doubleday.

SoftServe, N-iX, EPAM Ukraine, & Intellias. (2022). *Internal crisis management during the Russian invasion of Ukraine*.

Taleb, N. N. (2012). *Antifragile: Things that gain from disorder*. Random House.

Thurgood, K. (2023, July 20). *Healthcare leadership*. https://jindal.utdallas.edu/blog/the-leadership-moment-leading-in-times-of-crisis/

Wharton Executive Education. (2021, July 1). *After-action reviews: A simple yet powerful tool—Wharton*. https://executiveeducation.wharton.upenn.edu/thought-leadership/wharton-at-work/2021/07/after-action-reviews-simple-tool/

Acknowledgments

There are many people who deserve acknowledgments for their support in the creation of this book. James Kouzes, a renowned leadership author, has been respected and admired by both authors, who learned much of their leadership development strategies from him. Similarly, Jim Collins and Jeffrey Sonnenfeld are brilliant leader developers who impacted our thinking on the key topics. We would also like to acknowledge Ryan Flahive, Trinity Crompton, and Purvi Patel for their help and encouragement in taking on the significant commitment of authoring this book. The book would not have nearly the quality it achieved without the editorial genius of Kim Wimpsett, the Wiley developmental editor who assessed us, challenged us, corrected us, and put us on the right path to completion. Although she is not involved with this acknowledgment herself, Mariana Khomitska should receive a large amount of extra credit for the challenges she faced in authorship, with the need to move parts of her family from Kyiv to London, her work at all hours despite missile and drone attacks, the loss of power and internet as she tried to write, and the threat of death or injury from the Russian invaders of Ukraine. Her focus and intensity to share her knowledge with others is a unique treasure added to this book, and she should be an inspiration to us all. I know of no one braver or more committed to her work developing leaders than Mariana Khomitska. And of course, to our families who dealt with the disruptions and distractions caused by our authorship, thank you for your support.

About the Authors

Tom Kolditz is the managing member of Saxon Castle LLC, formerly the founding director, Doerr Institute for New Leaders at Rice University. Prior to founding the Institute, Tom designed the Leader Development Program at the Yale School of Management and chaired the Department of Behavioral Sciences and Leadership at West Point for 12 years. Brigadier General Kolditz has more than 35 years in leadership positions on four continents and received the Distinguished Service Medal, the US Army's highest award for service. He is a Fellow in the American Psychological Association and has published 2 books and more than 75 articles, including in the *Proceedings of the National Academy of Sciences* and the *Proceedings of the World Economic Forum*. His first book, *In Extremis Leadership: Leading as if Your Life Depended On It*, puts forth an original crisis leadership model. Tom has delivered more than 350 speeches worldwide. In 2017, he received the prestigious Warren Bennis Award for Excellence in Leadership, a distinction shared by noteworthy leaders including Benazir Bhutto, Doris Kearns Goodwin, and Bill George. A highly accomplished leadership coach, he was listed as #6 in the Coaching category in 2018 by Global Gurus, and in 2019, #24 in Coaching by Thinkers50, a UK management ranking group. In 2021, Global Gurus ranked Tom as #6 among start-up coaches and founders, and in 2023 and 2024, #12 and #13. In 2025, Thinkers50 awarded him the title of Coaching Legend, along with Mike Krzyzewski, the famous Duke basketball coach. He holds a BA from Vanderbilt University, three master's degrees, a PhD in psychology from the University of Missouri, and an honorary PhD from the Chicago School of Professional Psychology.

Mariana Khomitska is an organizational development and leadership expert with more than 19 years of experience in business education and executive development, including 13 years in managerial roles. She serves as Learning & Development Director at N-iX, where she leads global L&D strategy and develops leadership capability across countries in a fast-scaling international IT business. Her professional path unfolded during the COVID-19 pandemic, the full-scale war in Ukraine, the energy crisis, and periods of large-scale organizational restructuring. Working inside businesses during these disruptions, she not only designed leadership programs but operated within the uncertainty herself—managing teams amid sustained volatility, redesigning systems under crisis constraints, and supporting executives in real-time decision-making under pressure. Previously, she led talent and executive development initiatives at Academy DTEK, part of one of Ukraine's largest energy groups, and headed the Management Development Center at the European Business Association, supporting leaders across industries facing structural and geopolitical disruption. She developed dedicated programs for senior leaders on leading change in crisis, helping them strengthen adaptive capacity, maintain team stability, and make disciplined decisions in high-stakes environments. Her perspective is grounded in direct business practice: uncertainty is not an episodic challenge, but a structural condition of modern leadership—one that requires systemic thinking, resilience, and the ability to lead while conditions remain unstable. Her executive education at INSEAD, IE Business School, University of California, Berkeley, and the University of Sheffield informs her evidence-based approach to leadership in uncertainty.

Index